KOMA KULSHAN:

The Story of Mount Baker

KOMA KULSHAN:

The Story of Mount Baker

JOHN C. MILES

The Mountaineers • Seattle

The Mountaineers: Organized in 1906
". . . to explore, study, preserve, and enjoy
the natural beauty of the Northwest."

Published in the United States by The Mountaineers
715 Pike Street, Seattle, Washington 98101

Published simultaneously in Canada by Douglas & McIntyre
1615 Venables Street, Vancouver, British Columbia V5L 2H1

Book design by Elizabeth Watson.
Layout by Marge Mueller.
Maps by Katy Callaghan Huston.

Grateful acknowledgment is made for permission to reprint material from
Of Men and Mountains by William O. Douglas. Copyright 1950 by Harper
and Brothers. Reprinted by permission of Harper & Row Publishers, Inc.

Printed in the United States of America

Cover: Lowe party—the first photograph
taken on Mount Baker, by W.O. Amsden.

Page 2: South side of Mount Baker from Park Butte.

Library of Congress Cataloging in Publication Data

Miles, John C.
   Koma Kulshan.

   Bibliography: p.
   Includes index.
   1. Baker, Mount, Region (Wash.)—History. 2. Mountaineering—Washington
(State)—Baker, Mount, Region—History. I. Title.
F897.W57M55 1984   979.7'73   84-9781
ISBN 0-89886-073-3

To my father,
with thanks for
the direction
and support.

Climbing in icefall on Coleman Glacier

A mountain's life is a man's life multiplied by billions, but not a changeless infinity. The mountains call us, not to rest, but to work. A great peak is a frowning challenge, until we have scaled it; a strong and trusted friend thereafter. We can share in the life of the mountain; we can search its history until we are as old in knowledge as it is in experience; we can stand on its summit and be lifted up in spirit as if we had grown to its height and expanded in soul to the whole reach of a broadened horizon. The glaciers have carved a castle for us whose ceiling the sun emblazons with cubic miles of filmy gold; the winds fling banners from the bleak peaks; the winters of ages have piled our partitions; the summers of centuries have grown the pines for our bedposts, and God has scattered the firmament with stars, to give us courage by contemplating their infinity, to measure our pygmy finitude against the giant but also finite mountains. The torrents and the pines sing to us, the birds and the busy squirrels speak to us, the rocks preach to us, and the mind is at stress with the muscles as the soul breathes deep with the lungs. So the mountains enter into our lives as we enter into theirs. We are lifted up in the high places, not beyond ourselves, but to our best selves.

—*Chester Rowell, 1921*

Contents

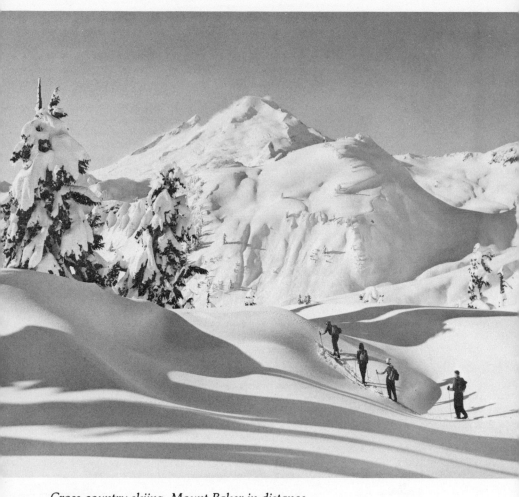

Cross-country skiing, Mount Baker in distance

Preface

Mount Baker is not a large mountain compared with the giants of the world, but it is a dominant landform where it stands. In northwestern Washington, people speak generally of the "Mount Baker Region," and refer to indeterminate areas according to their proximity to the high white bulk of ice, snow and rock towering five thousand feet above its foothills. On clear days our eyes are drawn to the volcano on the horizon. People in downtown Vancouver and Victoria, British Columbia, in Bellingham, Port Townsend, Everett, and even Seattle, Washington share its majesty. Mount Baker and other volcanoes scattered down the Cascade Range have been focal points for human attention and activity for more than a century.

The era of human interest in the mountain is but the blink of an eye in its history. Mount Baker is approximately four hundred thousand years old (or young, in view of Earth's four-billion-year history). Indians gazed upon Koma Kulshan, as some of them referred to it, for perhaps ten thousand years before white men came to the region. It was a place of forbidding mystery to them, though they climbed its flanks in search of mountain goats and berries. White men came late in the eighteenth century and noticed the mountain, but many years passed before anyone was motivated to venture upon it.

Mountaineering as a sport began early in the nineteenth century, and eventually climbers came to the glaciers of Mount Baker. The topographer Henry Custer passed close to it, as did prospectors, but they were busy with other pursuits. An Englishman, a man who climbed mountains for sport, finally rose to the challenge and climbed to Mount Baker's summit. Edmund T. Coleman and his companions were the first of thousands who have by now explored every possible route on the mountain's many glaciers and faces.

The story of Mount Baker is not, however, only the story of mountaineering on its heights. It is also a story of exploration and development, of prospecting and mining, of logging and government forest management, of promotion and preservation. It is a story of triumphs and tragedies, of Joe Morovits who explored and prospected and went away broke, of Harvey Haggard who trained and raced and won a marathon, of six college students who died in an avalanche. Above all, the Mount Baker story tells of a slow opening of a wilderness. It is a microcosm of the story of mountains in the American West. The story begins in a vast, virtually untracked wilderness, and it ends, at least in its telling here, with the wilderness still there but

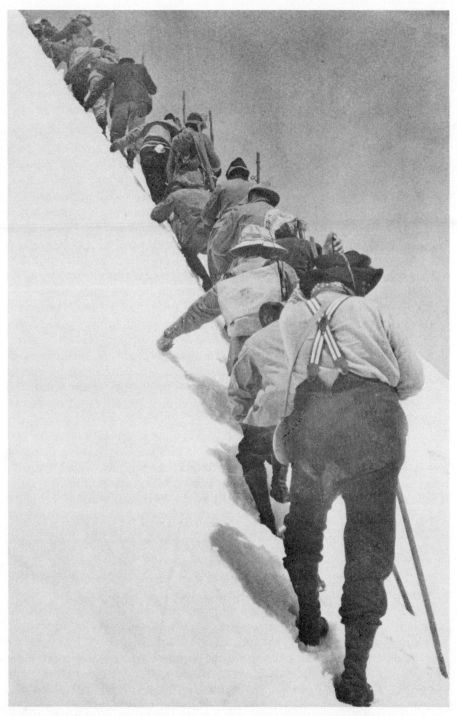

Alpenstocks were used for support by those on the 1908 Mountaineers summit climb.

greatly diminished. It begins in a time when the wilderness of North America was so vast that it seemed unlimited, in a time when wild country was an obstacle to be overcome. The story unfolds to the present, when wild country around Mount Baker is valued by many precisely because it is wild, when at least part of the people who know the place see in it values other than the minerals and timber that the early pioneers saw there.

The inspiration for this book came from Charles Finley Easton, the Bellingham jeweler who spent thirty years of his life as a part-time student of Mount Baker. Easton loved the mountain and wanted to share it with other people. To this end he wrote and talked endlessly to anyone who would listen. He promoted the idea of a Mount Baker National Park, actively so beginning in 1915. He compiled a huge scrapbook of Mount Baker information and memorabilia, Exhibit A in his efforts to promote a park, which was available for browsing at the Whatcom Museum of History and Art for many years after his death. I came upon Easton's "book" a decade ago; it provided the inspiration and resources to pursue a Mount Baker book of my own, for many of the same reasons that motivated Easton.

For Easton, climbing was joy. Studying the mountain gave him an excuse to climb it. He thought the mountain inspirational and worthy of attention for its unusual beauty. He was fascinated with the natural history of the place, particularly the glaciers, and wanted to know as much as he could about its many dimensions. I share all of these motivations with him.

Easton also seems to have been interested in promoting development of the Mount Baker region. He was a leader of the Mount Baker Club, the avowed goal of which was to attract public attention to the peak, principally through the Mount Baker Marathons, so that roads would be built and tourist trade would flourish. The idea of a Mount Baker Lodge was at least in part his. His promotion of a Mount Baker National Park was not borne of a preservationist leaning, as park promotion would be today, but because a park would attract a lot of attention and lead to tourist development and economic growth for the region. Many of Easton's dreams for the region have been realized, and I still advocate a park—but to stem the tide of development rather than enhance it.

Much of the Mount Baker story is, of course, about mountaineers and mountaineering. Mount Baker is not at the center of ordinary human enterprise, but is on the periphery. Most people who have encountered the mountain directly have done so for the fun and challenge of it. They have been mountaineers or skiers. Some have been pioneers of their sports—Coleman, Fred Beckey and Ben Thompson. Most have been in search of excitement and adventure who cared not that they followed in someone else's footsteps. For them, meeting the physical and emotional challenge of the climb and knowing that they had climbed that big mountain on the horizon has been enough satisfaction.

Most climbers have enjoyed their adventure and returned unscathed.

Rainbow Glacier, northeast side of Mount Baker

A few have not been so fortunate. Part of this story is tragic and heroic, of people being hurt or killed, and of people rescuing those in trouble. There have been remarkably few accidents in view of the multitudes who have walked upon Mount Baker in a century of activity. But the tragic part of the story must be told, if only to establish that a trip to this mountain is not to be taken too lightly.

This book was originally conceived as an encyclopedic treatment of Mount Baker. It was to deal with natural as well as human history. But natural history, fascinating as it is, would be distracting; it is the backdrop against which the human story is played. Mount Baker's natural history can be pieced together from several excellent sources available today, and can be left for comprehensive treatment in the future.

This project has been possible only with the help of many people, though only I can be held responsible for any errors that might appear. I am especially indebted to librarians at the Bellingham Public Library, the Western Washington University Library and The Mountaineers Library. The staff at the Whatcom Museum of History and Art were helpful, as were United States Forest Service people at the Glacier Ranger Station and the Supervisor's Office of the Mount Baker-Snoqualmie National Forest. The Mount Baker Hiking Club gave me access to their extensive scrapbooks, and Gary Haufle and Archie Lawson were especially helpful. George Mustoe, Tom Highberger, Fred Beckey, Alan Millar and Diane Cornell read the manuscript and offered helpful suggestions. Al Hugo offered inspiration and assistance with photographs. Brenda Hascall patiently typed the manuscript, and Laurie Winfield edited it. My wife and daughter tolerated and encouraged this grumpy author through the years that I struggled with this project. I thank them and all of the others who have made this book possible.

Edmund Coleman's depiction of the final few feet to the summit on his 1868 first ascent

The First Ascent

Mount Baker is the most northerly of those great cones which dot the Cascade range . . . like another "Snowy Olympus," it towers above, the silent sentinel of a solitary land. . . .
                                        —Edmund T. Coleman, 1869

Edmund Thomas Coleman was a tall and slender man of polished manner and gentle demeanor. A native of England, born in 1824, he was a librarian, a botanist and an accomplished artist. He was also a mountaineer, a charter member of the Alpine Club (London) who had climbed in the Alps and published work in which he described and illustrated the Mont Blanc massif. For unclear reasons, but most likely because he had exhausted his once considerable financial resources, he left England in 1862 and moved to Victoria on Vancouver Island, a community established nineteen years earlier as a Hudson's Bay Company fort. He claimed to have made the move because he was ". . . determined to leave the beaten paths of the European ice-fields for the unexplored heights of the west."[1]

If he had come to Vancouver Island to climb mountains, there could have been little doubt in his mind which mountain he should climb. There on the eastern horizon, gleaming white on cloudless days, like Mont Blanc, was Mount Baker. Other mountains could be seen in all directions, but none stood out so dramatically as this one. He wrote of it:

> Above all, it displays those towering masses, ever marked features of the earth, but pre-eminently conspicuous on this coast. These have their culminating

point in Mount Baker, one of the great peaks of the Pacific. . . . It
is remarkable for its beauty of outline bears a considerable re-
semblance in this respect to the Jungfrau, the queen of the Bernese
range of the Alps . . . . The height of this mountain is rendered the
more apparent from the circumstances of there being no other
peaks in the immediate neighborhood to dwarf it, and also from
the comparatively low height of the hills intervening between the
spectator and its base.

Perhaps Coleman came to Victoria rather than some other British colonial
town because of Mount Baker. He was familiar with the narrative of Captain Vancouver's voyage to the West Coast, with its engraving of Mount
Rainier. He might also have read Richard C. Mayne's description of British
Columbia, published in England in 1862. In Mayne's book was an engraving
of Mount Baker.[2] Whatever motivated him to come to Victoria, Coleman
found himself staring across at the mountain as he went about his daily
work as a librarian.

By 1866 he was ready to tackle Mount Baker. Time was pressing him.
He was forty-two years old. He was also "jaded and depressed, sick of the
monotonous round of my ordinary occupations." On July 19, 1866, Coleman crossed from Victoria to Port Townsend in the Washington Territory
to join a Dr. Robert Brown of Edinburgh, Scotland, and Charles Benjamin
Darwin, a United States magistrate assigned to the territory. The three men,
passengers in an Indian canoe, made for the delta of the Skagit River, thinking it would provide them with a route to the base of the mountain.

The river presented a few obstacles. Six miles upstream from its mouth
they came upon a huge log jam requiring three exhausting portages. The
brush was very thick and mosquitoes were at their midsummer peak. Coleman, Brown and Darwin persisted, making their way up the river to where
the Baker River comes in from the north. Knowing that their route must go
up this river, they sought guides among the Indians living there. But not only
were the natives unwilling to serve as guides, they refused to let the white
men go any farther. The party was forced to give up their attempt; Coleman
and Brown returned to Victoria.

Coleman was undaunted. Two days later he again boarded the steamer
to Port Townsend and once more set out for the mountain. This time he
went north to Bellingham Bay to ask local people about the best route to the
mountain. He discussed the prospects with Edward Eldridge, a local pioneer. Eldridge convinced him that the best approach would be up the
Nooksack River, which flowed from the very base of the peak. Eldridge
assured Coleman that he would not encounter unfriendly Indians as he had
on the Skagit; he knew members of the Lummi and Nooksack tribes living
along the proposed route and agreed to help procure Indian canoes and
other assistance.

Coleman party on the Nooksack River in their "shovel-nosed" canoes

Coleman recruited two local men to join him on the climb, both prospectors who had traveled close to the mountain six years before. John Bennett was a Scotsman who had arrived in the infant community of Sehome eight years before on his way to what he hoped would be richly rewarded labors in the gold fields of Canada's Fraser and Thompson rivers. (Sehome, one of three small communities on Bellingham Bay, would eventually become part of the city of Bellingham.) Riches eluded Bennett as they did so many gold-seekers, so he soon returned down the gold rush trail to Bellingham Bay to settle. Trained as a botanist, Bennett decided that one prudent path to riches would be to nurture his passion for plants into a business. He worked in the coal mines in Sehome, saved his money and bought land on which he established a nursery. This venture was progressing nicely when Coleman came along and, while visiting the Eldridges who lived next to Bennett's property, invited him to join the attempt to climb Mount Baker.

Bennett, Coleman and Eldridge went to the mouth of the Nooksack River, where they procured canoes and Indian guides and started up the river. A few miles upstream they encountered a log jam. Coleman undoubtedly hoped this one was not a bad omen. While the Indians worked the canoes around the jam, Bennett and Coleman walked to the cabin of John Tennant in hopes of persuading him to join the group.

John Bennett

Tennant, like Bennett, was interested in botany and was experimenting with plants on his homestead. His goal had once been gold; he had come west in the California rush of 1849. Now thirty-seven, Tennant had trained in his youth as a lawyer and been admitted to the bar in Arkansas. He found the legal profession unrewarding, so set off with thousands of others in search of adventure and fortune among California's gold-bearing gravels. When the gold fever subsided, he developed some skill as a surveyor and came to Sehome in 1856 to survey the coal mines there. He liked the area and stayed, acquiring a homestead on the banks of the Nooksack a few miles upstream from its mouth. Known as "The Black Prince" because of his tall and swarthy appearance, he was a tough and enterprising pioneer, probably impressing the more genteel Coleman as an ally who would considerably increase chances of success on the mountain.

Coleman, Tennant, Bennett and their Nooksack Indian assistants made their way up the river. Travel was difficult: the river was shallow and swift, not good for canoe travel. With great effort they struggled to the present site of Glacier and turned up milky Noochsakatsu (now called Glacier Creek) toward the mountain. Seven miles of extremely hard going brought them to the foot of what came to be known as Coleman Glacier, which they climbed, according to Coleman, to a saddle at its top. Tennant was taken ill at snow line, and Coleman and Bennett climbed the glacier. From the saddle the pair

John Tennant

21

Thomas Stratton

ascended northeastward up the cone, only to be stopped by "an over-hanging cornice of ice . . . [a] perpendicular wall. . . . A wall of ice." They knew they were near the summit, but the hour was late. They decided to retreat to the saddle with hopes of trying the last bit again the next day.

Their night was miserable "without blankets, and with only a small keg of cold tea to quench our raging thirst." Their "camp" was cold at nine thousand feet—both men "were forced to keep moving all night to keep from freezing." Despite their fatigue they tried again the next morning but again were stopped by the steep ice and conditions "very dangerous on account of avalanches and sliding ice." Coleman's disappointment, being denied success so close to his goal, can be imagined. He was probably near the top of what is now called the Roman Wall, a mere two hundred feet below the summit. Unable to circumvent its difficulties because of fatigue and lack of provisions and time, Bennett and Coleman returned once more to the saddle, where they planted what they had hoped would be the summit flag, along with a "pain killer" bottle, and turned back down the mountain. Rejoining Tennant and their two guides, they enjoyed a wild ride down the Nooksack, marveling at the skill with which the Indians ran the rapids. Safely reaching the mouth of the river, Coleman was unable to find Indians to paddle him to Victoria. He spent two weeks with Eldridge, sketching scenes of the area, and finally returned to Victoria on September 5. He had spent a month and a half trying to climb Mount Baker.

Two years later Coleman was back on the shores of Bellingham Bay. Indians had brought him and David Ogilvy through the San Juan Islands from Victoria by canoe. Ogilvy, reportedly an experienced climber in his early thirties, had been hired by Coleman to assist in what he intended this time to be a complete ascent of Mount Baker. These two were joined at the home of Edward Eldridge by Thomas Stratton, the Customs Inspector in Port Townsend, whom Coleman had invited to join the expedition. The adventurers enjoyed the frontier hospitality of the Eldridge family and their friends. When it was time to depart, a farewell ceremony was held, described by Coleman:

> When the maidens fair bade 'good-bye,' I asked them to pray for us; but one, more lively than the others, observed that we should be so much nearer heaven we ought to pray for them.

Coleman departed Whatcom in the company of Stratton, Ogilvy, their Indian boatman and Eldridge, who accompanied them for thirty miles before turning back. Bennett did not join them. The memory of the pain endured in the bivouac two years before was still strong, and he decided that he preferred the amenities of the lowlands to high adventure. The party proceeded to the mouth of the Nooksack River, where they once again enlisted

Coleman and party portaging the canoes

the skillful navigation services of Nooksack Indians and their "shovel-nosed canoes." Four Indians were to accompany them on the adventure; two, Squock and Talum, had been with Coleman on the earlier Nooksack River attempt.

On August 7 they started up the river. When they reached the log jam, Coleman left the portaging to the Indians and again paid a visit to John Tennant. Despite Tennant's infirmities during the climb two years before, Coleman had been impressed by him. He asked Tennant to join the party, and Tennant agreed. They returned to their canoes and continued up river. The water was high and the going difficult in places. Another log jam required a portage. It was strenuous poling through riffles, but they made good progress the first day and pitched camp for the night on the riverbank. Here Coleman discovered "defects in our culinary arrangements." He noted that the whole party had only one plate and spoon between them and wryly described the menu:

> Breakfast—Tea, bread, bacon.
> Dinner—Bread, bacon, tea.
> Supper—Bacon, tea, bread.

The intrepid group made do with what they had and got on their way early the next morning. They passed the last outpost of civilization, the homestead of a Colonel Patterson, and the village of the Nooksack Indians, and again camped. Continuing, they encountered forks in the river and chose to go up Nuxtig'um or the Middle Fork of the Nooksack. This would take them to the south of Mount Baker, instead of up Cuwae-lic (North Fork), where Coleman had struggled two years before. Squock and Talum recommended Nuxtig'um, "alleging that a day's journey would bring us to the head of navigation, and that in the three days' land travel between that and the snow line we would find occasional elk trails, and reach a point where the ascent was more easy." They struggled up the swift and shallow river assisted by a Nooksack Indian hunter, made three portages and poled through "twenty-seven riffles or rapids." These difficulties convinced them that camp that night would be the "head of navigation," so they cached their canoes and provisions, taking enough bacon, tea and bread for ten days. They set out on foot, hefting heavy packs, on August 11.

> . . . we plunged into the forest along the bank of the river in order
> to reach a ford some twelve miles up. With difficulty we made
> about a mile an hour, over fallen trees, under old logs, down steep
> ravines, over high rough rocks, and through close-set jungle.

The going was indeed difficult. Thick, almost impenetrable growths of vine maple required strenuous detours. Prickly spines of devil's club tore at them

Edmund Coleman's Mt. Baker Attempts 1866 & 1868

and frayed their tempers. According to Coleman, Stratton's high spirits carried them along, and they finally pitched "Camp Fatigue" on the river bank where the waters of what came to be known as Clearwater Creek join the larger stream.

Next morning they continued, encountering more troubled travel. Uncertainty increased their vexation; they were unsure where to turn uphill from the river toward the mountain. After their second exhausting day they pitched "Camp Doubtful" beside another roaring tributary of the river.

Squock and Talum were dispatched on a scouting mission next morning. Coleman got out his sketchbook, while Stratton, Tennant and Ogilvy went prospecting. The Indians returned late in the day with word that they had found a way up to snow line. They had also killed some marmots to supplement the expedition's monotonous diet. The prospectors had found no sign of gold. Despite the hopeful news, Coleman could not sleep:

> The expectation of five years' solitude and exile was about to be realized, or else delayed until another season had wearily come round. The struggle maintained in the land of the stranger ap-

proached its denouement. Was I to stand a conqueror upon the mountain summit, or return with the memory of defeat to behold it from the shore of my island home.

He finally dropped off to sleep, but dreamed of dangers. Suddenly he started awake:

My companions were sunk in sleep around me, the campfire had died out, the night was cold and chilly. The noise of the river, deafening during the day, was like thunder in the stillness of the night. The thought that it had thus fought its coarse [sic] night and day, throughout the rolling centuries, filled me with awe. It seemed like some remorseless being madly bent on destruction, and was to me an emblem of unrelenting power and inexorable will.

The following morning, August 14, the forests were enveloped in thick fog, but Coleman felt much better once he got moving uphill. They climbed up through forests of hemlock and fir and gained the top of the ridge which was, according to Coleman, about five yards broad. The fog drifted by, opening occasionally to reveal a glacier far below them to the northeast. Worn out, they camped again, calling this one "Camp Hope." They were at an elevation of about six thousand feet on Marmot Ridge. Burning with thirst, with no potable water near their camp, they sent the Indians off with all of their pots and pans to find some. While they waited for the water they "were cheered by observing that the clearing of the fog had revealed two magnificent rocky peaks or 'aiguilles,' as they are termed in Switzerland, to which we gave the names of 'Lincoln' and 'Colfax.'" The Indians returned with some water they had located five hundred feet below camp. The men downed their bacon, tea and bread and turned in.

The fog continued to surround them the next day, the fifteenth, so they decided not to climb. Coleman stayed in camp and sketched while part of the group set out hunting to supplement the boring rations. Hoping for bear or elk, of which they saw sign on the ridge, they returned with several marmots. According to Coleman, Stratton concocted a stew which "was consumed with a relish which none but hungry mountaineers can experience." Stratton himself, in recalling the meal, was more restrained, noting that the marmots "were acceptable as a fresh meal, though not very palatable."[3]

When they awoke at dawn on the sixteenth the fog lay in the valley below, but the mountains were clear. They could see the cone of Mount Baker, the Black Buttes and the Twin Sisters Range to the south. Coleman compared the latter peaks in shape and color to the "Aiguilles Rouges" of Chamonix in the French Alps. They broke Camp Hope and continued up the ridge, which gradually flattened out, and established their final camp at

Coleman's party ascending the Middle Fork of the Nooksack

7,054 feet, according to Coleman's aneroid barometer. It was only 9 a.m. but too late to climb. Coleman continued his sketching. Ogilvy went hunting and bagged a ptarmigan. Coleman notes that Tennant and Stratton

> . . . went to try some creepers [crampons] which had been made for the occasion, being doubtful that they would answer; they also reconnoitered the proposed route. They returned in high spirits . . . declaring that with the creepers they could walk up the slopes of snow as firmly as on a hillside.

The party organized for the next day's bid for the summit.

At 5 a.m. they set off with provisions for twenty-four hours. The weather was clear, their spirits high. By 6:30 a.m. they reached the end of the ridge, where the Indians bid them well and set off back to camp. The four climbers looked out across the glacier and immediately disagreed about the best route to their objective. Coleman was for following the ridge to the top of Colfax; his experience in the Alps had taught him that this was the safest way to go, along the ridge. But Stratton, with "a happy ignorance of the dangers of concealed crevasses or chasms and the frailties of snow-bridges," set out on his own track right across the glacier below Lincoln Peak, unroped.

Coleman, Tennant and Ogilvy talked the situation over and decided to follow Stratton who was by now out of sight among the ridges and hummocks of the glacier. They roped up and set off, "in considerable anxiety concerning Stratton." Occasionally they caught a glimpse of him far ahead as they slowly made their way across the névé below Colfax Peak. Coleman was tired, his age telling on him by his account, but he plodded along. They made their way to the saddle between Colfax Peak and the main peak without incident. Mounting a ridge of rotting volcanic debris, they looked down the southern side of the mountain. It was time for rest and refreshment:

> Ogilvy pounded some ice, and, with the aid of brandy, made a cocktail; it was very acceptable, and was christened the Mount Baker cocktail. Its fame reached Victoria, where it was reproduced at one of the bars; and, aided by the exhibition of a veritable piece of rock from the summit, attracted thirsty crowds .... fortified by this refreshment and an hour's rest, we made for the top of the saddle by the northern side of these rocks.

A long ridge of "a deposit resembling mud" stretched above the saddle for several hundred feet upward toward what is known today as the Roman Wall. Its top is a flat rocky bench; here they caught up with Stratton, who was feeling rather sickly due to the "sulphurous exhalations" issuing from the crater a short distance to the east. Despite his nausea he was ready for the final slope. Coleman describes the section that had frustrated him and Bennett two years earlier:

> Around the summit of the peak is a perpendicular wall of ice about thirty or forty feet in height, terminated on the left or northern end by a knuckle of rock, which can be plainly seen from the Sound. The only passage we could discern through this barrier is on the left, between the knuckle of rock before-mentioned and the wall of ice. The face of the peak is scored with deep furrows, made by avalanches of ice which have fallen from the summit. The peak rises about 1000 feet higher. It commences with a gentle slope, and gradually becomes steeper, until near the summit it is about 60°.

They started up, encountering no problems at first, but as the slope steepened it became necessary to cut steps. Stratton was going strong again, so he took the lead.

> The axe was passed on to Stratton, who plied it with vigor and skill. While thus engaged he got a great fright. Having heard a dull, grating sound, he looked up and saw a mass of frozen snow, about 12 feet square, moving down toward him. Paralyzed with terror, he was about to warn us, when it stopped. Even at this height there were crevasses. Into one of these Tennant sank, but managed to extricate himself.

They gained the knuckle of rock, rested there for a short time, and walked onto the summit plateau. It was 4 p.m. Coleman's dream was realized.

The summit was white, with no rocks showing. The view was obscured by a pall of smoke from forest fires which "lay like a reddish cloud beneath us." Stratton describes the scene:

> What an indescribable feeling passed over us! No word was spoken, as we stood with clasped hands, contemplating the majestic grandeur of the scene. At such a time and such a place one feels the spirit of inspiration that led the Psalmist to exclaim, "Great are Thy works, O Lord!"[4]

They sang an appropriate religious song, then planted the Stars and Stripes and sang a patriotic song. A flask of brandy was produced, and everyone interested in the expedition was duly honored. Looking across the summit snow, Coleman saw a small peak on the far end. Wanting to be sure that they were truly on the highest point of their mountain, they trudged across to it and duly planted the flag again.

Coleman sketched while the others looked around the summit. They found a vantage point where they could look into the crater. Stratton described their view as "an awful sight. Down, down—all dark and sulphury, with green, black, red and yellow sides."[5] Wisps of steam rose from vents in the crater. Though impressed by what they had seen, they did not tell Coleman of their discovery, presumably fearing he would want to sketch the scene although the hour was growing late. The sun was dropping rapidly in the west, and they "stood upon a little island, surrounded by a boundless sea of vapor."[6]

Coleman's sketching done, they roped up and set off on their descent, prompted by fears of being benighted on the mountain as Coleman and Bennett had been two years earlier. The steep upper section of the Roman Wall, the descent of which had been haunting them on the summit, proved easy; they walked and slid quickly down to their packs at the bottom of the wall.

Coleman's depiction of climbing onto the summit plateau

They left the summit at 6 p.m. and pressed downward. Coleman notes

> The sun was already sinking, so we had no time to lose. Urged by
> the fear of having to pass the night on the mountain, we plunged
> after Stratton down the slopes, across snow-bridges, by walls of
> ice, as if pursued by a fiend. Vain were my remonstrances, fearful
> of an accident, but my companions hurried on in a manner that
> would have sent a Swiss guide into fits. Such a helter-skelter mad-
> brained party was never seen on either Mont Blanc or Mont
> Rosa.

As darkness closed in around them, they lost their way and were forced to
backtrack until they found their tracks of the morning ascent. Coleman was
exhausted, but his younger companions urged him onward till at 9 p.m.
they arrived at the point where they had left the ridge and taken to the snow.
Two more hours of effort in the darkness finally brought them to their high
camp, where the Indians had a large fire going and were anxiously awaiting
them. Refreshed by bowls of tea, they turned in. Even as they did so, the
wind began to rise and a storm moved in upon them. Coleman, in rare

understatement, noted that "as we turned round in our blankets, we felt thankful that we were not on the mountain."

The next day was devoted to rest and sketching, and then they set out on the return journey. It was August 19. Instead of retracing their steps, they decided to take advantage of the high open parklands as much as possible. They descended to the west along Grouse Ridge rather than down their ascent route on Marmot Ridge. One camp on the ridge and a long day brought them down Clearwater Creek and back to Camp Fatigue. The return canoe trip was fast and exciting, and by August 22 the group was back on Bellingham Bay. They had been two weeks on their journey.

The first ascent of Mount Baker seems to have been the high point in the life of Edmund T. Coleman.[4] He had come out from England, among other things, to find adventure and to satisfy his passion for mountains. He had come with artistic and perhaps even literary ambitions as well. Upon his return to Victoria he wrote a lengthy account of his Mount Baker adventure and sent it, along with his sketches, to one of the major publishing houses in New York. They published his article in *Harpers New Monthly Magazine,* one of the leading periodicals of the time. It was illustrated with woodcuts based on his sketches. Coleman had not only advanced himself as a mountaineer, but also as an artist and writer.

Though there is no evidence that Coleman succeeded in any major mountaineering ventures after Mount Baker, he appears once more in North American mountaineering history. In August of 1870 Coleman joined two young men on what turned out to be generally credited as the first complete ascent of Mount Rainier. He was not, however, with Hazard Stevens and Philemon Van Trump when they reached the summit. Coleman was older and more cautious than his companions, fell behind on the difficult approach to the mountain, and never even made it to snow line. Stevens and Van Trump were unkind to Coleman in later descriptions of their adventures, and he was undoubtedly disappointed in this unhappy end to his climbing career.

After this fiasco Coleman continued his travels in the Pacific Northwest for several years. He visited Portland in 1871, then journeyed south to San Francisco. In 1873 he traveled to Chicago on the newly completed Union Pacific Railroad, then continued home to England. Little is known of his life there, but he published a number of articles about his travels and explorations in the American West and continued writing about mountains. He died in London on May 24, 1892, at the age of 68.

2

Early History of the Mount Baker Region

Farthest away in the west, as near the western sea as mountains can stand, are the Cascades.... Kulshan, misnamed Mount Baker by the vulgar, is their northernmost buttress up at 49 and Frazer's River. Kulshan is an irregular, massive, mound-shaped peak, worthy to stand a white emblem of perpetual peace between us and our brother Britons.

—Theodore Winthrop, 1862

The first humans to have any contact with Mount Baker were the Indians who lived in sight of it. Many of them undoubtedly gazed up at it from their lowland homesites. The Lummis, for instance, lived in the San Juan Islands; on clear days the mountain dominates the eastern view from these islands. Few Indians ventured onto the slopes of the mountain itself, though the Nooksacks who lived to the west of its base, and the Upper Skagits to the south and east, hunted game and gathered berries in its forests and subalpine meadows. There is no evidence that Indians walked the glaciers or climbed the mountain.

How long were the Indians in the vicinity of Mount Baker? The archaeological record is not conclusive, but it seems to indicate that Indians first lived in the Puget lowlands some eleven to twelve thousand years ago.[1] They probably lived in the upper Skagit region at that time, perhaps along the Nooksack as well. They inhabited the region continuously up to historic times, gradually increasing their ability to utilize the rich resources of their environment. Coastal groups based their hunting and gathering life-style on sea mammals and salmon, while inland groups like the Nooksack and Upper Skagit hunted big game like deer, elk and mountain goat and fished the rivers for salmon.

Pursuit of the mountain goat probably brought the Nooksack and Ska-git Indians closest to Mount Baker. They undoubtedly ate goat meat, but the goat's most important product was its hair, long and thick, great for winter warmth. The Indians gathered this "wool" to weave their Salish-style blankets. It was not always necessary to kill the goat to get its wool; in spring and early summer the goats shed their wool in great clumps, leaving it hanging on bushes. Perhaps they thrash around in the brush intentionally to rid themselves of their overly warm winter coats. Goats have predictable behavior patterns, so the wool could be found in the same general areas every year. The Nooksacks and Upper Skagits probably knew well the goat paths and the likeliest shedding areas. True, they killed the goats for their meat and hides when they could, but they also simply gathered the hair from these areas. Either hunting or gathering wool would have brought the In-dians to timberline in places with full view of Mount Baker's upper slopes.

Goat wool was important to upriver Indians, for it gave them some-thing to exchange with lowland tribes, who valued warm blankets but had no direct access to the goats. The Nooksacks and Upper Skagits could trade their wool for marine mammal products to which they in turn had no access. The Nooksacks jealously protected their goat-hunting grounds, which ex-plains the anger of Edmund Coleman's Indian guides of 1868 upon discover-ing evidence of Indians' poaching game on Marmot Ridge, southwest of the mountain. The guides thought the poachers were probably Thompson In-dians from British Columbia; two years earlier a Thompson had been killed by a Nooksack hunter for poaching in that area. Because Skagit Indians also hunted goats on Mount Baker, precise territorial hunting lines must have been established.

The Indian groups had different names for the mountain. Early settlers thought the Lummis referred to it as *Koma Kulshan*, which has been vari-ously translated. Charles Buchanan, writing around 1913, mentions that:

> Kulshan is a Lummi word indicating that the summit of the peak has been damaged, or blown off by an explosion ("just as if shot at the end," as one Indian explained it). This word is used of other things damaged or supposed to be damaged in a similar manner, and it is not limited at all in its use to Mt. Baker. The term does not mean "The Great White Watcher," or "The Shining One," as com-monly interpreted.[2]

Recent linguistic research offers another explanation for the origin of the name Koma Kulshan. The source of *Kulshan* may be the Nooksack *kwélés,* "to shoot." Incorporated into a phrase descriptive of a common hunting practice, it would have been *kwómae kwelsáen,* meaning "go up high or way back in the mountains shooting." The proper Nooksack name for the peak was *kwéq smáenit,* which is translated as "white mountain."[3] Early settlers struggling to understand Indian languages adopted the phrase as the proper name and, perhaps not accurately distinguishing Lummi and Nooksack language in this case, accepted Koma Kulshan as the Indian name for the peak.

The Upper Skagits referred to the volcano as *t'kuba,* meaning "snow all around." The mountain was one of their guardian spirits, one reputed supplier of the berries that grew abundantly on its slopes.[4] Such spirits were "owned" by members of the Upper Skagit community and brought various attributes to their owners. There is no record of what attributes *t'kuba* brought to its owners, who acquired it through a prescribed quest in their youth. The guardian spirits spent most of the year with others of their kind, according to the Skagits in a world outside the human one. They would come on particular occasions when their human owners needed help, and at least once each year, when a special ceremony was held for them. This spirit world was central to the traditional religion of the people who lived close to the mountain, though the mountain spirit itself does not seem to have been of unusual stature or significance.

Aboriginal people of the Northwest Coast and elsewhere often developed stories and myths to explain the world around them. Charles Buchanan recorded one such story, a Lummi tale explaining the origin of Mounts Baker and Rainier and other familiar geographic features.

> In the olden days, so the old folks tell us, Kulshan was a fair and handsome youth who grew apace to man's estate and then espoused two wives. One of these wives fully equaled her husband in beauty—she was the favorite wife and her name was Duh-hwähk. She bore Kulshan three fine sons. The other wife was no match for Duh-hwähk in beauty but she was very amiable, very kind, and very attractive in manner. This wife was named Whäht-kwāy. Eventually it came about that the kindness and consideration of Whäht-kwāy so completely won over her husband that she supplanted Duh-hwähk in the affections of Kulshan. This, of course, aroused furious fires of jealousy and resentment in the breast of Duh-hwähk, who constantly kept the entire household in dissension and strife by means of her temper and her jealousy. Finally Duh-hwähk resolved to regain Kulshan by artifice. Relying confidently on her beauty and on her former firm sway over her husband she conceived the plan of feigning to desert him. So, one day, when it happened that by chance she found Kulshan in amiable and mellow mood and more pliant to

her purpose, she complained to him of the coldness and harshness with which she, Duh-hwähk, had been treated in the household, even more by Whäht-kwāy than by Kulshan. She assured her husband that she loved him but that the burden was more than even her great love for him could bear and that unless he soon changed these conditions she must leave him and take with her all of her possessions. Kulshan resolved to be master in his own household and without hesitation informed Duh-hwähk that she could go as soon as she chose and as far as she liked. Duh-hwähk was dumbfounded by this unexpected reply. She felt that she must make things appear to him in a more serious light. She felt confident of his love and sure that at the last Kulshan would relent. Indeed, she could not believe that he would really permit her thus to desert him. Founding her faith on this imagination she gathered up her possessions and made ready to go at once. She prepared her pack thoroughly, putting therein plentiful supplies of berries, fruit, sweet bulbs, and even of beautiful flowering plants of many varieties. Thus amply provided with all that she desired she then said farewell and fared forth, leaving her three children behind. The children bewailed the going of their mother and with many lamentations besought her to remain. This greatly pleased Duh-hwähk at heart for she now felt assured of melting the indifference of Kulshan. She was sure that he would call her back before she had been able to go any very great distance. With this in mind she managed to set forth on a course that would take her the longest way. So also she traveled down the valley between the mountain ranges so as to be always in sight of Kulshan as long as possible, thinking to give him ample opportunity to recall her. She had not gone far, however, before she realized her mistake and richly repented her hasty action. So, as she went along, she would ever and anon look anxiously back. Her heart surged tumultuously with a fond hoping and a vain longing to see Kulshan wildly signal for her return—how she hoped that he would do so! Alas, she had gone too far for that, perhaps, and, besides, many little hills and valleys now intervened between her and home where she had left Kulshan and the weeping children. Therefore, she must needs climb the knolls and pick out the highest hills from which to gaze back with longing eyes and sinking heart. Standing on the very summits of these hills she would strain with all her might, up to the very tips of her toes, seeking some sign from her loved husband. Sometimes she fancied she was not quite high enough and she would raise to her tip-toes and stretch forth her head in anxious gaze, yearning all the while and striving all the while to be just a little taller. This oft-repeated wish

and effort soon began to have its effect upon her and she forth-
with began to grow taller. At last she had gone so far that she must
of necessity make camp. She selected as her stopping place one
that seemed most satisfactory to her because from it she could
have a clear view of her dear home so foolishly and uselessly
abandoned. Here she removed her packs and cast the contents
broadcast, blessing the place with all the stores of fruit, of berries,
bulbs, tubers, and beautiful flowering plants of many wonderful
varieties, all of which she had taken away from Kulshan. There,
looking ever and longingly northward, Duh-hwähk remains to
this day and you may see her if you wish—look to the south and
east—it is Mount Rainier where Duh-hwähk cast them forth
before she herself became the mountain. To the north lies the
deserted husband, Kulshan, robbed of fruits and the beautiful
things which Duh-hwähk took with her. Look to the north and
you will see him, but the white man calls him Mount Baker, not
Kulshan! All about Kulshan, too, you may see the deserted and
weeping children. [5]

There were powerful spirits in the mountains, which is perhaps why Indians never ventured high on Mount Baker's flanks, nor on those of its volcanic counterparts. When Stevens and Van Trump enlisted an Indian guide,
Sliuskin, to help them climb Mount Rainier, he would not go beyond snow
line. "In the lake lives a mighty demon. If you should reach the top, the
demon will seize you and kill you and throw you into the fiery lake." [6] He
was amazed when they returned safely two days later and reported that they
had been to the summit. Similarly, Squock and Talum would not venture
onto the snows with Edmund Coleman. Some Indians reported Mount
Baker to have a fiery and dangerous aspect:

Kulshan once got so mad that a big piece fell off and slid way
down the mountain. This made a big fire and lots of noise. Kulshan and Shuksan became black all over. The waters in the rivers
became black and warm. Fish came floating down the rivers
cooked. Lots of Indians and animals fled. Next year most of them
went back again. Since then Kulshan has never been mad. [7]

This was probably an account of a volcanic eruption of the mountain.

Mount Baker also appears in a legend of the Squamish, an Indian group
that lived along Howe Sound, in British Columbia, not far to the north. The
mountain is central to their account of the great flood or deluge, stories of
which have been found in the traditions of many Pacific Northwest Indian
groups. Faced with the prospect of the flood, the Squamish men built a giant
canoe, and the women wove a strong rope with which to anchor it. They
fastened the rope to the canoe and to a large rock, then placed their babies

and young children in the boat, along with food and fresh water for many days. The mother of the youngest baby and the bravest young man also embarked as guardians of the children.

As the floodwaters rose, the rest of the group was drowned, but the canoe safely rode the rising waters for many days. Then, as the rain subsided and the waters began to fall, the man saw land. It was the summit of Mount Baker. Cutting the anchor rope, they paddled to the mountain and landed on its flanks.

> When the waters had gone down and the land below was dry, they made a new camp. They built their lodges in the region between the Fraser River and the Georgia Strait, in sight of Mount Baker. The children lived and grew up. Through them the Squamish people were saved.[8]

The Indians lived with Mount Baker for thousands of years before white people appeared on the scene. With their passion for "discoverers," white students of the mountain's history have speculated about who might have been the first white person to see it. Charles Finley Easton, a long-time student of the mountain and the first historian of the Mount Baker Club, expended a lot of energy on the question. He drew an elaborate map and located on it what he called the "theoretic horizon" from which an early explorer might have been able to see the mountain in good weather. Beyond that horizon the curvature of the earth would have made seeing it impossible, no matter the weather. Then he plotted the courses of the explorers who sailed the Northwest Coast as best he could.[9]

All the earliest explorers were beyond the horizon. The Russians, who established themselves in the Aleutian Islands in the middle of the eighteenth century, were working their way along the coast in search of furs. To the south, the Spanish had occupied Mexico and explored northward to San Francisco Bay. Perceiving that the Russians might thwart their territorial ambitions, the Spanish dispatched an expedition in 1773 to establish their dominion along the Northwest Coast up to 60° north latitude. Juan Perez reached the vicinity of the Queen Charlotte Islands but was forced to turn back southward by the onset of scurvy in his crew. At 49°30' north latitude he found a protected harbor and anchored in what is thought to have been Nootka Sound, on the western coast of Vancouver Island.

The next year, another Spanish expedition was dispatched from San Blas, Mexico. Under the command of Bruno de Heceta, and accompanied by Bodega y Quadra, the expedition was to sail to 65° north latitude, then explore southward and take possession of the coast for Spain. They anchored off the coast of present-day Washington, and landing parties went ashore to take possession. Seven members of one of the parties were killed by Indians, probably at Moclips, an inauspicious start for these, the first white men known to stand on the shores of Washington. Heceta sailed south after this incident and returned to his base in Mexico.

A few years later, Captain James Cook of the Royal Navy sailed up the coast and landed at Nootka Sound. Bad weather had prevented him from sighting the Strait of Juan de Fuca, but his visit to the Northwest Coast was significant—it brought England into the region. Though Cook was killed the next winter by natives in Hawaii, his ship continued exploration of the Alaska coast and then proceeded to China, where the immense value of the furs the crew had collected along the Pacific Northwest Coast became evident. Furs would provide the incentive for much future British activity in the region.

Word spread about these rich fur resources; English and American traders and sailors appeared. In July of 1787 the English maritime trader William Barkley sighted the entrance to a great inlet, the Strait of Juan de Fuca. Its presence was also noted by an American trader, Robert Gray, but neither of them ventured very far into the strait. The British trader Captain John Meares also sighted the strait in 1788 and named it for the Greek Apostolus Valerianos, also known as Juan de Fuca, whom he thought had been the first European to visit the strait in 1596. It seems safe to say that none of these explorers penetrated Easton's theoretic horizon and saw the mountain, though they were laying the groundwork for those who soon would.

It was in 1790 that the mountain was recorded for the first time by a European. The Spanish had established a settlement at Nootka in 1789, and when word of the existence of the strait reached Spanish officials, they sent an expedition to chart it. Ensign Manuel Quimper of the Spanish Navy was in charge; his first pilot was Gonzalo Lopez de Haro. Quimper's sloop probed its way along the north shore of the strait to the present site of Victoria, British Columbia, from which the mountain is visible on a clear day. The party crossed the strait to Dungeness Bay. Quimper's second pilot, Juan Carrasco, took his longboat eastward and sighted Rosario Strait and Deception Pass. After a few days charting Dungeness Bay, Quimper proceeded out of the strait, crossing first to the southern shore of Vancouver Island, then coming back south in search of fresh water. He made the first explorations of the north coast of the Olympic Peninsula.[10] In the course of all this Quimper and his party spent weeks in places where Mount Baker would be visible to them. Though Quimper made no reference to the mountain in his

Charles Easton's drawing of Mount Baker

journal of the voyage, Haro's manuscript chart of the Strait of Juan de Fuca includes a sketch of a prominent peak in the Mount Baker region entitled "La Gran Montana del Carmelo."[11] Thus was Mount Baker "discovered."

Another Spanish party came through the strait in June of 1791 under the leadership of Juan Francisco de Eliza. They explored the San Juan Islands to the Strait of Georgia and probably saw the mountain, for they spent the full month of July in view of it. They encountered Indians on Padilla Bay and Point Roberts, who told them that other white men had preceded them in large ships and even over land. Eliza's party recorded nothing about Mount Baker.

Spain had sent two vessels into Nootka in 1789 to fortify and protect the harbor, still trying to retain their claim to dominion over the region. In trying to protect the harbor, they created an international incident by seizing ships flying the English flag. This event ultimately led to a treaty signed in Madrid in 1790 between Spain and England called the Nootka Convention. In the treaty Spain conceded to England that she could trade anywhere on the Pacific Coast north of the forty-second parallel, the current boundary between Oregon and California. England could also set up posts and settlements anywhere that Spain had not already occupied. Finally, reparations would be made for English ships and other property taken at Nootka. In 1791 the British Admiralty commissioned George Vancouver as commander of an expedition to survey the Northwest Coast and to proceed to Nootka to meet with the Spanish representative there for the purpose of carrying out the terms of the Nootka Convention.

Vancouver left England on April 1, 1791, with two ships, H.M.S. *Discovery* and H.M.S. *Chatham*. He passed around the Cape of Good Hope to southwestern Australia, New Zealand, Tahiti, and then to the Hawaiian Islands, where they spent the winter. On March 16, 1792, they sailed for the Pacific Northwest, arriving on the coast of Washington on April 28. There they met the American fur-trading ship *Columbia* commanded by Captain Robert Gray. They learned what they could from Gray about the Strait of Juan de Fuca, sailed into the strait with a gentle wind and clear weather and made for Dungeness Bay, on the south shore of the strait, Quimper's anchorage two years earlier. At about 5 p.m. Third-lieutenant Joseph Baker, on board the *Discovery*, happened to look to the northeast:

> About this time a very high conspicuous craggy mountain, bearing by compass N. 50 E. presented itself, towering above the clouds: as low down as they allowed it to be visible it was covered with snow; and south of it, was a long ridge of very rugged snowy mountains, much less elevated, which seemed to stretch to a considerable distance . . . . the high distant land formed, as already observed, like detached islands, amongst which the lofty mountain, discovered in the afternoon by the third lieutenant, and in

compliment to him called by me MOUNT BAKER, rose a very
conspicuous object, bearing by compass N. 43 E., apparently at a
very remote distance.[12]

Thus, though Haro had named the mountain on his chart in 1790, it fell to an
Englishman to give the peak the name it bears today. Haro's chart went unpublished for eighty-two years, by which time the Spanish had long been
gone from the region. In the official narrative of Vancouver's voyage,
printed in London in 1798, there appears the first published reference to
Mount Baker.

The man for whom the mountain was named remains a rather obscure
figure. Third-lieutenant Baker was from an old Norman family of Bristol,
England. His father, Captain Valentine Baker, had enjoyed a distinguished
Royal Navy career, from which he had retired to become Harbor Master at
Bristol. Joseph was his fourth surviving son and aspired to follow his father
in a naval career. Captain George Vancouver was very impressed with the
young man and eventually gave him command of the *Discovery*. Baker
eventually became a captain, too; he died unmarried in 1817 in Bristol.

Mount Baker was one of Vancouver's first "discoveries." His ships lay
over at Port Discovery for sixteen days for refitting and repairs; Vancouver
and some of his men explored southward and eastward. On May 18 the
Chatham explored northward, and the *Discovery* entered Admiralty Inlet.
The two ships commenced thirty-eight days of exploration of what Vancouver named Puget Sound (after another of his lieutenants, Peter Puget). In
the course of these explorations the party observed another large mountain
to the south and east; Vancouver named it Mount Rainier. His explorations
in the area completed, Vancouver sailed north on June 24 and accomplished
the first circumnavigation of Vancouver Island. He anchored at Nootka
Sound where he met with Bodega y Quadra regarding the Nootka Convention, according to plan. Vancouver and Quadra could not reach agreement
as to how the terms of the convention were to be carried out, but other
negotiators three years later did so, resulting in Spanish abandonment of
Nootka. Thenceforth the Spanish were to play no further role in the history
of the Mount Baker region.

Mount Baker had been discovered, recorded and named but was not to
figure centrally in the lives of Americans and Europeans for seventy-four
years. During this time the United States and England wrangled over who
should possess that part of North America north of the Columbia River. The
English hoped to control all land south to the river, and American aspirations extended as far north as 54°40' north latitude—nearly to southeast
Alaska. After a period of joint occupancy during which the present state of
Washington was controlled by the North West Company and then the Hudson's Bay Company (the two merged in 1821), the Mount Baker region
became American in 1846. England decided that the country between the

An Easton sketch of Lieutenant Joseph Baker and
George Vancouver's ship, the Discovery

Columbia and Fraser rivers was not worth warring with the United States. The rich fur resources of the region were exhausted, so the Hudson's Bay Company agreed to move its western headquarters from Fort Vancouver on the Columbia River to Vancouver Island, at the present site of Victoria. After much negotiation the forty-ninth parallel was agreed upon as the international boundary, beginning at the Rocky Mountains and running due west to the center of the channel separating Vancouver Island from the continent, then following the center of that channel southerly, bisecting the Strait of Juan de Fuca to the Pacific Ocean. There would be minor disputes, but the central territorial question was resolved. Settlement on both sides of the border could proceed.

There is no evidence of any special interest in Mount Baker from its naming until Edmund Coleman began planning to climb it in the 1860s. During the first half of the nineteenth century fur traders and trappers undoubtedly viewed the mountain, but they seldom kept records of their exploits; no reference to Mount Baker by such men is known. They traveled the Fraser River (beginning with Simon Fraser in 1808) and sailed among the San Juan Islands, but the rugged country surrounding Mount Baker did not attract them. Indians brought furs from near Mount Baker to Fort Langley, established in 1825 on the Fraser River, or to Fort Victoria after 1843. Some Skagit Indians even traded furs as far away as the Hudson's Bay Company's Nisqually House, established near present-day Olympia in 1833.[13]

The lowlands west of Mount Baker began to be settled at mid-century, after establishment of the international boundary. In 1850, Isaac Ebey came to Whidbey Island and became the first permanent settler in lower Skagit territory. Captain Henry Roeder and Russell Peabody became the first settlers on Bellingham Bay late in 1852. In 1849 there were only 304 white people in Oregon Territory north of the Columbia River, but soon thereafter gold seekers disappointed in California came north—the 1850 census showed an increase to over one thousand people.[14] By 1853 there were enough settlers and enough political justification to warrant creation of a separate Washington Territory. By 1855 the pressures of settlement were sufficient to motivate the territorial government to seek a treaty with the Indians. In the infamous Point Elliot Treaty, representatives from many Puget Sound Indian groups (excluding the Nooksacks, among others) ceded their land in return for reservations and other benefits. This treaty was to cause great trouble for the Indians around Mount Baker, but of course helped the process of white settlement.

The largest white community in the region was Fort Victoria on Vancouver Island. From this base the English sought to colonize what was to become the province of British Columbia, to insure that it remained English and did not go the way of the Columbia River country. For various reasons settlement north of the international boundary, except at Victoria, was slow until the late 1850s. Before the Fraser River gold rush of 1858, the population of Victoria was approximately five hundred, mostly Hudson's Bay Company employees, past and present, and their families.[15]

The white population of the Puget Sound lowlands near the mountain grew slowly during the 1850s. Coal mines opened at Sehome (now part of Bellingham) and provided employment; there was a lucrative coal market in San Francisco. Indian trouble on Bellingham Bay and throughout Washington Territory led to the establishment of Fort Bellingham in 1856. Sixty-eight soldiers commanded by Captain George E. Pickett arrived in August of 1856. Pickett was later to achieve fame as a Confederate army general.

The greatest boost to settlement was the Fraser River gold rush of 1858. In February of 1858 the Hudson's Bay Company shipped eight hundred ounces of Fraser River gold dust to the United States Mint in San Francisco. Word of its source got out, and thousands of stampeders came to Bellingham Bay and other places with access to the gold-producing river country. A rough trail running north from the village of Whatcom on the bay, long used by Indians trading in the Fraser River valley, was touted as the easiest way to the strike. The gold soon petered out, and the Whatcom Trail did not turn out to be such an easy route. Frustrated gold seekers began to filter back into Washington Territory, their hopes for riches dashed. Some went to work in the Sehome coal mines and eventually helped settle the Bellingham Bay and Nooksack River areas.

One recorded venture into the Mount Baker region during this period is that of the Northwest Boundary Survey, a party of English and American surveyors who set out to establish the precise location of the international boundary in 1858. While the surveyors took their readings and laborers cut a swath through the forests and over mountainous country to mark the boundary, the American topographer Henry Custer explored the country on both sides of the line. Custer, his survey companions and his Indian guides ranged between the Fraser and Nooksack rivers, climbing peaks and exploring valleys. One foray took them through the low pass between what is now called Columbia Valley and Silver Lake, then down the outlet stream of the lake to the Nooksack River. Turning up river they passed the confluence of the North Fork of the Nooksack and Glacier Creek, the site of the modern community of Glacier, just a few miles from Mount Baker. Continuing on, they traveled up the North Fork to where it is joined by Ruth Creek, then followed this to its head at Hannegan Pass. An Indian trail, presumably one used by the Nooksacks for berrying and hunting, made travel up the river a straightforward venture. Custer saw Mount Baker on some of his climbs. He knew he was near it on his trip up the Nooksack River but had neither the time nor the means to attempt climbing it.

A second foray close to the mountain was that of the Tennant-Lane Expedition of 1860. Two of its five members were John Tennant and John Bennett, who would later return to the upper Nooksack with Edmund T. Coleman to attempt to climb Mount Baker. The 1860 group had no interest in the mountain, but was after gold. From Bellingham Bay they made their way to Lake Whatcom, then rafted up the lake and laboriously climbed over the hill to the east and descended into the valley of the South Fork of the Nooksack. Panning the river bars, they found some color, so hopefully, but with difficulty, they made their way upstream. In the end they found little gold and returned discouraged. The most significant outcome of their expedition was that Tennant and Bennett became interested in the upper Nooksack region and learned something about it. They also met some of the Nooksack Indians who lived there, and were on good terms with them. Eight years later, when Coleman arrived at the growing community on Bellingham Bay and inquired about companions to accompany him, Tennant and Bennett would be mentioned and eventually agree to go on Coleman's historic adventure.

3

Prospectors and Pioneers

Many and wonderful have been the changes which have taken place beneath the shadow of our beloved snow-capped mountain —our Mount Baker, whose lofty peaks were seen but dimly through the towering branches of the giant trees which lined our rivers and filled our valleys at the time of which I write.
—Robert Emmett Hawley,
Nooksack Valley Pioneer, 1945[1]

Edmund Coleman was an anomaly in the Washington Territory. An educated, urbane, esthetic gentleman, a painter—he was obsessed with climbing mountains, and particularly Mount Baker, merely for the sake of the climb and the pleasures of mountaineering. No others with this obsession appeared in the Mount Baker region for many years after his pioneering climb. It was twenty-three years, in fact, before the next climber stood atop the peak.

Events in the surrounding lowlands during this period were to make the mountain accessible to the next generation of mountaineers. Settlers slowly moved up the Nooksack and Skagit River valleys. They first established themselves at Mount Vernon on the Skagit in 1870; by 1877 logging had begun and settlers had moved as far upriver as Hamilton, due south of the mountain, to mine coal. In the Nooksack Valley settlers were moving on to the fertile and flat land along the river. By 1877 a road had been built from Whatcom on Bellingham Bay to Nooksack Crossing near the modern town of Everson. White settlers were in clear view of the mountain, but had enough to do just to clear the great trees

An early-century homestead, perched beside the Nooksack River

off their land so that they could plant and tend their crops. Settlers generally were family oriented, the men unwilling and uninterested in any unnecessary risks that might jeopardize the welfare of their families. They leaned occasionally on their shovels and axes to admire the view but made no move toward the mountain.

Another breed still wandered the land, however, and these did venture into the hills. They sought not adventure but gold, though they usually found more adventure. In 1877 a party went up the Skagit River in search of gold, probed up the Baker River, found little there, and continued on up the Skagit. They explored widely, panning in likely places, and by 1879 were washing payable quantities of gold out of creek gravels. Their success led to typically inflated stories of a bonanza at Ruby Creek on the Upper Skagit, and there was a bonafide rush there in 1879-80. Throngs of "argonauts," as they were called in those days, estimated at more than a thousand, braved the hazards of the river and the mountains. Most were frustrated, but the Ruby Creek Mines, though many miles east of the mountain itself, proved to be an important stimulant to the opening of the Mount Baker region.

There was gold-rushing in the Nooksack River and Mount Baker region as well. No record exists of prospecting in the vicinity of Mount Baker

Packtrain, loading up for a trip to the mines, early in this century

after the Tennant-Lane expedition of 1860 until Thomas Barrett ventured into the South Fork Valley in 1878. Barrett, a gregarious fellow who kept the company store for the Sehome coal mines for many years, retired from storekeeping to try homesteading. Finding farm work a hard and rather lonesome grind, he returned to civilization, to Sehome, where he bought the coal company's saloon, which he knew had always been a lucrative business. What Barrett did not know when he bought the saloon was that the coal company was planning to shut down. When they closed the mines, the would-be entrepreneur was broke. Like many others in similar straits he decided to try to recover his losses by finding the gold rumored to be somewhere along the South Fork of the Nooksack. Pulling together an outfit with two companions, Barrett and associates explored, by his account, some one hundred miles of country up the South Fork. Barrett's luck remained poor; after six weeks of struggling with the rugged country south and west of Mount Baker, the seekers limped back into town, their clothes in tatters, their pockets empty. Barrett decided farming had its virtues after all and lived out his years on his farm with its modest but steady living.

Prospectors are like gamblers. Despite repeated frustration they remain eternally hopeful and cannot shake the lure of the strike. The rich bar may be just around the next bend in the creek, the mother lode in the mountains just upstream. Countless Tom Barretts went into the Mount Baker country with high hopes and came back in tatters. There were always more argonauts outward bound. Two prospecting parties of the 1880s, though they found little gold, contributed significantly to the exploration of Mount Baker.

William Henry Dorr arrived in Whatcom County from Iowa in 1882 and established a homestead. One day he talked with a Nooksack Indian who claimed to have been hunting on Mount Baker's north side. According to Dorr, the Indian told him "that there was a place at the head of a stream of water a short distance below where it came out from under the snow over on that side of the high mountain where it directly faces the rising sun in the long summer days, where there were heaps of gold."[2] The Indian knelt and drew a crude map in the sand. Dorr decided to investigate.

Carrying sixty-pound packs, Dorr and a friend set out for the mountain. They were guided by the Indian's map, which Dorr had transposed from sand to paper. It took them four days of hard going up the North Fork until they reached the mouth of Glacier Creek. At times they had to walk in the riverbed to avoid the thick tangle of undergrowth along the bank. After a night's rest at the confluence of the two streams, they followed Glacier Creek for a mile, then climbed steeply uphill east of the creek to the top of Skyline Divide, which the Indian had said would provide a route to the region of the mountain where the gold was to be found.

They struck the ridgetop, a delightful place resplendent with flowering meadows and clumps of pointed firs. Up this ridge they went, after a pleasant camp among the flowers, from Skyline to Chowder Ridge, across a small glacier (Hadley Glacier) to a campsite on the north side of the slope where Cougar Divide meets Chowder Ridge. They knew they were close to their objective, for the mountain loomed just above them. Crossing Dobbs Creek, they walked to the very east end of Chowder Ridge and saw what must have been the site of the Indian's Eldorado, where Barr Creek emerged from beneath the Mazama Glacier.

> Here we located the Siwash gold mine. There was a sparkle of glittering mica about the edges of the water and mixed with finer grit in the eddies, just such a showing as might be expected to impress the untutored mind of the savage, but very disappointing to the prospector.[3]

Still, they staked their claim, named it Siwash, and panned and explored the area. Their efforts went unrewarded, so they returned to their camp.

It is easy to imagine Dorr looking up at Mount Baker and telling his companion that since they had done better than half the work of climbing it, they might as well go the rest of the way. The view would be good, and

Route of Dorr's 1880s summit attempt, as seen from Skyline Divide

maybe it would be fun. They set off up the northeastern ridge, commonly known today as Cockscomb Ridge.

> There was no bad climbing aside from the numerous broad and very deep crevasses but the rise was rapid being fully 30 per cent grade on the average. We reached a high point or spire of lava overlooking a steaming crater on this northeast slope but we were caught in a snow squall and forced to retrace our steps.[4]

The spire of lava is today called the Cockscomb, at approximately 9700 feet elevation. Good weather would not have assured them of success, for the spire is extremely crumbly volcanic rock and could not have been surmounted. With no climbing equipment or experience the pair could not have bypassed the rock on either side, for steep ice and crevasses make that a challenge even today.

They turned back, but left their mark on the mountain. The "steaming crater" they spotted below them was not really a crater but a group of fumaroles. Today these are known as the Dorr Fumaroles, and plumes of steam can still be seen rising from them at the eight-thousand-foot level.

Another party was on the mountain during the summer of 1884, this one on the opposite side from Dorr. They, too, were prospectors who went up the South Fork of the Nooksack. But according to L.L. Bales, who described the trip in an interview and article, they also intended to try to climb the mountain. Bales and four companions left Whatcom on June 16 and made their way to the South Fork, up which they traveled for a week. They went slowly, presumably looking for gold and exploring the unfamiliar country. Bales broke out his fishing line from time to time, supplementing their trail food. He reported fishing to be excellent, even in the very upper reaches of the river. They climbed a minor peak of the Three Sisters group, and eventually made their way to timberline on Baker's south side.

Three members of the party decided to climb, the other two to hunt mountain goats. The three climbers crossed a large glacier, which Bales refers to as the head of the Baker River, and "ascended the mountain from the southeast side."[5] One climber dropped out, and Bales and Victor Lowe continued upward. "After several hours of very difficult climbing, Mr. V.V. Lowe and myself succeeded in reaching the summit."[6] They enjoyed the view, then descended to their companions and returned to Whatcom by way of the Middle Fork of the Nooksack.

Victor Lowe

But did they make the summit of Mount Baker, as Bales led the readers of his 1890 *Pacific Magazine* article to believe? One student of the mountain's history, Harry Majors, credits Bales and Lowe with the second ascent, but there is reason to doubt.[7] An account of the climb was published in *The West Shore* in 1884, condensed from the account that appeared in the *Whatcom Reveille* shortly after the party returned from their adventure. In this account Bales and Lowe "persevered, and by constantly encouraging each other and resting every few steps, finally reached the apex of the eastern summit, about twenty-five feet lower than the dome-shaped summit visible from the Sound, and 150 yards distant from it. They were too exhausted by their efforts to attempt the other apex."[8] This "eastern summit" sounds suspiciously like Sherman Peak, which is approximately seven hundred feet below the actual summit and slightly over one-half mile away from

An Indian home in the Nooksack region

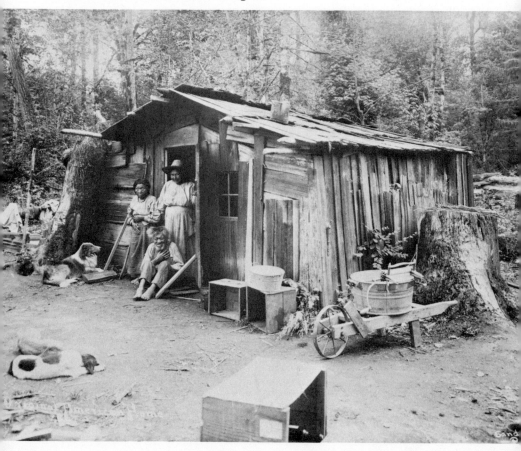

it as the crow flies. Perhaps at this point the climbers exaggerated their closeness to the summit, though admitting that they had not made the last little bit to the top. Another possibility is that they emerged onto the summit plateau and gazed across at the small prominence on its northeast corner. Exhausted, they did not go this short additional distance. Either way they did not reach the summit.

There is also a descriptive detail in Bales' 1890 account that lends some credence to the Sherman Peak possibility. He says that he and his companions crossed "a large glacier, the head of Baker River, and ascended the mountain from the southeast side."[9] If the party came up the moraine known as Railroad Grade, crossed Easton Glacier to Squok Glacier, then struck for the highest point above them, they could have inadvertently found themselves atop Sherman Peak. If visibility was poor, as it often is, they might have climbed Sherman Peak thinking that they were on their way to the summit, only to gaze exhaustedly across at the higher peak from the point they had achieved.

A 1906 article in the Seattle *Post-Intelligencer* lends some credence to the argument that Bales and Lowe were atop Sherman Peak rather than Mount Baker itself. Frank Teck, in reviewing climbs of Mount Baker, notes that "Lowe and Bales claimed they had reached the summit of Sherman Peak June 29, and discovered an immense extinct crater, a thousand feet deep and half a mile in diameter. . . ."[10] Thus Bales and Lowe probably made the first ascent of Sherman Peak, the pointed summit of the east rim of the crater. For whatever reason, Bales made an erroneous claim to the second ascent of Mount Baker in his 1890 account.

Sixteen years after Coleman's party made footprints across the summit plateau, several parties had followed new routes to the mountain's summit region. The lure of gold drew them to the area, but once they were close to the mountain it cast its own spell upon them. And they had responded to the challenge. The 1884 achievements were a sign of adventures and adventurers to come.

Another seven years were to pass before Mount Baker's summit snows were to beckon, but meanwhile events were unfolding that would make the mountain more accessible and clear the way for successful future ascents. Central to this part of the story are the Ruby Creek mines on the upper Skagit River mentioned earlier. When the gold rush up the Skagit was peaking, the economy of the young communities on Bellingham Bay was in need of stimulation, and the idea for a road from Bellingham Bay to the mines was conceived. The entrepreneurs reasoned that such a road would bring mine-related business to their community. When the idea surfaced in 1879, there was no road beyond the Nooksack River at Nooksack Crossing, a few miles from the Bay, but that was no deterrent to aspiration.

There was nothing but talk about the new road for many years. In 1886 a party of six men traveled much of the route which road promoters were discussing. One member of this party was Banning Austin, who was to figure prominently in later road developments. Austin's group left Whatcom on July 12 in search of a new route from Whatcom through to the upper Skagit and "to do some prospecting for a mining and milling company."[11] Their route took them up the North Fork to Wells Creek, then up this creek until they could ascend a peak bordering the stream, probably Barometer Mountain or a promontory on Lasiocarpa Ridge. Their travels from there are uncertain, but somehow they made their way back to the Nooksack upstream from where they had left it and then continued up the river to Ruth Creek. Austin's party eventually reached the Skagit River after twenty-eight arduous days of travel over extremely rough terrain. They had experienced the country that any road from Bellingham Bay to the Ruby Creek mines would have to traverse. We would expect that they would have brought a discouraging report to the would-be road builders back in Whatcom, but this does not seem to have happened.

Great Excelsior Stamp Mill

Banning Austin's fanciful map of the proposed road to the Ruby Creek Mines. The map failed to include the rugged Picket Range.

Years passed after Austin's expedition, but the road idea remained strong in many minds. Slowly the trail up the Nooksack was made into a wagon road. By 1893 the road extended to the present site of Maple Falls. That year the Washington State Legislature, at the urging of local politicians, created State Road District Number One and provided $20 thousand for the work, with other money to be contributed by the counties involved. The act provided for a state road through the Cascade mountains north of Mount Baker to connect eastern and western Washington. The road was to go up the Nooksack River north of Mount Baker to a point on the Columbia River opposite the town of Marcus in Stevens County.

Banning Austin was hired to survey the route, since he called himself an engineer and knew the country as well as anyone. Austin, E.P. Chace, H. Hall and R. Lyle went up the North Fork to the boggy area called Breckenridge Bottoms, just downriver from the mouth of Ruth Creek. They could see a low pass to the south, west of Mount Shuksan. Austin, perhaps remembering the jumble of mountains from his previous trip, decided to investigate this pass, hoping for an alternative. The pass, which came to be called Austin Pass, proved discouraging, so they returned to the river. Replenishing their supplies, they climbed up Ruth Creek again to Hannegan Pass (named for one of the road commissioners, J.F. Hannegan). Dropping to the Chilliwack River, they went downstream to Brush Creek, then up Brush Creek to Whatcom Pass. Continuing, they traveled down Little Beaver Creek, then climbed a ridge from which they could look down the valley of Big Beaver Creek. Convinced they had found a feasible route, they returned to Whatcom with enthusiastic reports.

Construction began immediately. During 1893 road work reached six miles above Nooksack Falls, and the trail was improved to within a few miles of Hannegan Pass. As the summer passed, problems with finances and authority developed, resulting in the resignation of two of the road commissioners. A new commission was appointed and a new reconnaissance launched. The utter futility of trying to build a road over the proposed route to the Ruby Creek mines and Eastern Washington was finally recognized, and the project was scrapped. It was also clear by this time that the Ruby Creek mines were of no great importance; business minds on Bellingham Bay had new schemes for improving their economy, most of which involved railroads.

The North Cascades road fiasco provided the impetus for road building well up the valley of the North Fork of the Nooksack River, thereby considerably improving access to the Mount Baker region. After 1893 it was easier to get to the mountain, and even more prospectors and mountaineers would travel into the region. And the road ultimately was built. The idea born in 1879 would reach fruition in 1972 with the opening of the North Cascades Highway which, ironically enough, would not go up the Nooksack but the Skagit River.[12]

Gold fields map of 1902 mining heyday

Late nineteenth-century map showing claims and townsites in the Twin Lakes area during the peak of prospecting activity

While this wildly impractical road building scheme was occupying some people, others were quietly going about the business of settling the country around the mountain. The first settler moved into the valley of the South Fork in 1883, and others soon followed. A townsite called Livewood was laid out at the mouth of Skookum Creek in 1885. There was rumor of gold in the area, and cheechacos and sourdoughs, as newcomers and oldtimers in the prospecting business were respectively called, rushed in to investigate. *The Reveille,* a paper which had recently started publishing in Whatcom, ran the headline, "RICH MINES ABSOLUTELY FOUND ON THE SOUTH FORK OF THE NOOKSACK!!" The editor wrote:

> Now and then for years an occasional nugget or a little dust has been found, but NOW the boys, excited by recent discoveries, will flock to new diggings. The Cariboo Mines are nowhere, compared to the new find, and diggings are only twenty or thirty miles from Whatcom—on the South Fork of the Nooksack and Whatcom will soon rival the famous Leadville in its palmiest days.[13]

The editor overstated the case a bit, as he often did, and by the end of 1885 the truth was known—there was no bonanza on the South Fork. Still, men had scoured the area, and the pace of settlement increased.

Settlers gradually established themselves on the North Fork as well. The first one set up housekeeping at Kendall in 1884, at Boulder Creek in 1889, and at Glacier in 1893. Railroads were on everyone's minds in the late 1880s, for they promised great growth and business opportunities, particularly if they were tied to national rail lines. The great aspirations of regional rail promoters were never to materialize, but by 1890 rails were approaching the Mount Baker country from the south, west and north. The days of epic trips *to* the mountain, when the approach equalled the climb for adventure and difficulty, were rapidly fading. The mountain was opening, and what would be called an "epidemic of mountaineering" was about to begin.

4

The Mountaineering
Epidemic

*The mountains are fountains not only of rivers and fertile soil,
but of men. Therefore we are all, in some sense, mountaineers,
and going to the mountains is going home.*
                                                    —John Muir, 1874

The year 1891 began what Charles Finley Easton, Mount
Baker's earliest historian, called the "epidemic of mountaineering." Suddenly people were responding to the sporting challenge of the mountain. The population of the Puget Sound region
was growing rapidly. Access to the mountains was improving.
Many climbers were ascending Mount Rainier, among them John
Muir in 1888. Eloquent writers like Muir were extolling the
wonders of mountains and mountain travel for their own sakes.
The era of pioneering was coming to a close in the Pacific Northwest, and men and women with a love of outdoor adventure
turned to sports instead of frontier exploration.

In late June of 1891 a party of eight local men, six from the
town of Blaine and two from Sumas, set out to prospect the lower
reaches of the mountain and to climb it if possible. They made
their way over dusty, rough roads to Maple Falls, then followed
the trail to the mouth of Glacier Creek, where they camped.
Above them rose the small but precipitous Church Mountain. No
one had climbed this little mountain before, as far as they knew.
They accepted the challenge, struggling up steep tree-covered
slopes to slide paths of tangled alder, then through alpine
meadows to the short rock scramble leading to the summit. The

climb was strenuous, but the party was young and strong. They enjoyed the trip immensely. From the top of Church they could look southward and see the summit reaches of Mount Baker gleaming in the sunshine, and they renewed their resolve to climb it.

From their viewpoint it looked as if the easiest approach to the mountain was up Glacier Creek. Its milky water indicated that it flowed from the glaciers. Early summer runoff made the stream roar and leap; they could hear it rolling large boulders beneath its rough surface. They headed upstream, staying as close to it as they could, and found the traveling very difficult. At one point the creek travels through a deep gorge, where they had to negotiate very steep sidehills. They kept at it. After several days of struggle they eventually emerged from the nearly impenetrable brush into a huge basin into which tumbled large glaciers directly off the western and northern sides of the mountain. They had gained little elevation, but they were at last free of the hostile vegetation. Settling down for a rest, they gazed at their gleaming objective far above. Their resting spot was just below the snout of Roosevelt Glacier at an elevation of approximately four thousand feet. Their only predecessors on this approach had been Coleman, Bennett and Tennant on their attempt in 1866, when they reached the upper slopes of the mountain but could not find their way over a large crevasse onto the summit.

It was about noon and the group was exhausted. They decided to make camp right where they were. Steep gravelly slopes rose north and south of them, and as they reclined they heard a rockslide. Looking up they saw the cause of the slide: several mountain goats were browsing leisurely across the slope above them. The goats had not detected their presence, so two of the men, E.H. Thomas and Richard Smith, grabbed their rifles and set off up the hillside after fresh meat. The going was steep and difficult as the way quickly turned into unstable gravel that provided very poor footing. Clouds of dust rose above them as they climbed, and they could not avoid dislodging rocks and boulders, which bounded noisily down the slope. The goats, alerted to danger by all the commotion, started to slip away. The men climbed faster and harder, using their rifles as third legs for stability.

Suddenly Smith's rifle discharged, wounding him in the upper part of his right arm, severing an artery. His heart was pounding hard from the exertion, and blood spurted brightly from the wound. Smith lost consciousness and tumbled headlong down the slope. He fell two hundred feet, sustaining more injuries in the fall. His companions rushed to his aid but could do little for him. His shocked friends buried him on Bastille Ridge and abandoned their aspirations to climb the mountain. Thus inauspiciously did the "epidemic of mountaineering" begin.

A thousand feet above this party, several miles to the south, another group was bent on climbing the mountain. Members of this party later claimed that they heard the shot that killed poor Smith. The fact that there were two parties trying to climb the mountain at the same time indicates how times were changing in the Mount Baker region. This group of eight men (among them V.V. Lowe, who had accompanied Bales up Sherman Peak five years earlier) had come up the Middle Fork of the Nooksack River. Upon reaching Clearwater Creek they had followed it to its headwaters, then climbed the divide between Clearwater and Glacier creeks. They were camped high on this divide when they heard the fatal shot.

Unaware of the unfolding drama nearby, they proceeded to make the second complete ascent of the mountain. They went up Grouse Ridge, traversed over to Heliotrope Ridge, then made their way onto Coleman Glacier. Traversing beneath the Black Buttes, they gained the saddle between Colfax Peak and the summit, then climbed the Roman Wall to the top. They had little difficulty. The weather was warm, the wind light, the view unobstructed and they were elated. They planted two poles in the snow, unfurled an American flag and struck heroic postures for the first photographs ever taken on the summit. Wandering around, they looked over the sides of the summit plateau, gazed into the crater and generally enjoyed themselves.

An 1892 party on the summit, gathered around the stake (in center) left by the 1891 LaConner party

Historic Routes to the Summit

Glacier Creek

Skyline Divide

Deadhorse Creek

Cougar Divide

Dobbs Creek

Bar Creek

Ptarmigan Ridge

Chowder Ridge

Camp Kiser

Bastille Ridge

Mazama Glacier

Kulshan Cabin

Roosevelt Glacier

Rainbow Glacier

Rainbow Creek

Coleman Glacier

Park Glacier

Marmot Ridge

Summit

Black Buttes

Crater

Boulder Glacier

Park Creek

Wallace Creek

Deming Glacier

Sherman Peak

Easton Glacier

Middle Fork Nooksack River

Railroad Grade

Sulphur Moraine

.._.._.. Glacier Trail (Marathon Route)
.... La Conner Party - 1891
._._._. 1906 Mazama Route
_ _ _ _ 1909 Mazama Route
Deming Trail
(Marathon Route)

63

Reluctantly and uneventfully, they left the top and descended to their camp, though badly sunburned and suffering from snow blindness. "Smith and Whitetruck," Lowe wrote afterward, "had their faces in unrecognizable shape and they could not see for some time . . . we were all affected more or less and are not over it yet."[1]

This climb marked the beginning of modern mountaineering on Mount Baker. Some members of the party had come quite a distance to make the climb. Mount Baker's first photographer was W.O. Amsden from Seattle, who was to make another important climb one month later. He made the ninth successful ascent of Mount Rainier, taking some historic photographs on his way.

Photographers had to be dedicated in those days; their equipment was so heavy and awkward. Amsden used an eight-by-ten view camera on Mount Baker. A year before Arthur Warner had carried such a photographic outfit to the top of Rainier to take the first photographs there. Warner's camera was eighteen inches long, with a body twelve inches square. The lens had an aperture of f.22 and lacked a shutter. Exposures were made by plucking a black cap from the lens and replacing it again. Warner's outfit, with its tripod, glass plates and other items, weighed over fifty pounds.[2] It is likely that Amsden used a similar outfit. Climbing mountains like Rainier and Baker was no easy task back in those early days; the photographers who carried such loads and went to such pains to record the early climbs were truly remarkable people.

The next party to climb Mount Baker in 1891 came at the mountain from an entirely new direction: east, from Baker Lake. The group members —all from LaConner, a small community near the mouth of the Skagit River—were J.O. Boen, "Leader and Photographer"; Sue Nevin and William Land, "Artists"; Charles Beilenberg, "Guide"; Alex Beilenberg, "Cook"; S.W. Bailey, "Scribe"; and Robert Woods, "Camp Attendant."[3] Obviously, everyone had his role to play on this expedition. In mid-August they traveled by stage from LaConner to trailhead, then followed the trail up Baker River to Baker Lake. This was a hike of about twenty miles to a smaller lake than is present today; the modern lake was created by a power dam. It was pleasant at the lake, cool and calm in the wilderness solitude of beautiful August days. They enjoyed the lake so much that they spent three days there relaxing and summoning the courage and ambition to undertake the really strenuous part of their trip. They were camped near the lake at approximately seven hundred feet elevation and were facing a climb of ten thousand feet to the summit. The mountain was only a few miles west of their camp, but they had to make a laborious bushwhack over entirely untrodden ground to reach timberline.

Finally they set off upward. The going was as difficult as they expected it to be. They had to wind among giant trees and climb over or around huge logs lying on the forest floor. They had to traverse steep sidehills, cross rush-

Sue Nevin, the first woman to climb Mount Baker

ing streams, and cut their way through tangles of devil's club, vine maple and other vegetation. Fortunately they were in the cool shade most of the time. It took two difficult days to reach timberline at the base of Boulder Ridge, about four thousand feet. A day of rest and recovery was needed before they could push on to the summit.

> Monday morning the tug of war commenced, and for nine and a half hours we did as hard climbing as any people ever did. We followed as near as possible up the east side of the mountain, part of the time over the brim of a yawning crater where one misstep would have carried us over to death in the abyss below.
>
> As we neared the top we had to get down into crevasses and work our way through them and with the ax cut steps in their opposite sides and climb out again only to find other crevasses ahead of us. We were finally compelled to take to the heights of projecting rocks because of the depth of melting snow and the thick grouping of the crevasses.
>
> When we had thus ascended to within about one hundred feet of the summit we encountered a crevasse in the snow 25 or 30 feet across and 50 or 75 feet deep, the opposite wall of which seemed to be a perpendicular face of ice. Right here we all sat down disheartened and discouraged for it seemed impossible to overcome this final barrier.
>
> Robert Woods, resolving to make one more effort, left the party and found the end of the crevasse where he was enabled to let himself down. After an hour's persistent work with his ax he succeeded in getting up the other side of the crevasse. He was then lost sight of but soon the air was rent with his triumphant whoops, which assured us that he had reached the summit. We followed his steps and, under the inspiration of refreshed courage we were at his side a half-hour later—on the summit, 4:30 o'clock, Monday, August 24.[2]

They had made the first ascent of the Boulder Ridge–Boulder Glacier route, negotiating some rather tricky crevasses in the section above the ridge. Sue Nevins, the "brave Iowa girl . . . a vivacious young woman just out of her teens" had climbed strongly and, seemingly to the surprise of her male associates, "stood the fatigue of the trip fully as well as did her companions."[5] She was, of course, the first woman to climb the mountain and would be the only woman to climb it until many did so with the Mountaineers party of 1908. The Boen group did not stay on the summit long because it was very cold and late in the day. They returned the way they had come and reached their timberline camp at 8 p.m. A new and soon-to-be popular route on Mount Baker had been discovered.

J.M. Edson and P.J. Harris, photographed by E.A. Hegg on their first ascent of Twin Sisters, 1891

Mount Baker was not the only mountain in the region attracting some attention in 1891. The Twin Sisters Range, a group of small rocky peaks to the southwest, was visited in August by J.M. Edson, P.J. Harris and E.A. Hegg. This trio made its way to the mountain by way of the Park and Saxon Post Offices to the confluence of Skookum Creek and the South Fork of the Nooksack River. From there they struck eastward for several miles, keeping to the north of the creek. The going was typically rough. There was no trail, and vegetation was dense. Finally, they reached a meadow at the head of a branch of Skookum Creek at the base of the rocky high point of the range, the 6932-foot South Twin. From there they were able to work their way upward through a narrow gorge, then over boulder fields and talus until they encountered snow and steep rock. The crux of their climb was the summit itself, where "the only foothold is the narrow, irregular shelves and jutting points of rock to be found on an almost perpendicular cliff. This was surmounted with much difficulty and danger, tearing clothing and lacerating fingers...."[6] The dunite rock on these crags is unusually abrasive, as all climbers since this first threesome have discovered. Once on the summit they could gaze across a deep cirque at the North Twin, and beyond that to the great panorama of Mount Baker. A glacier wraps around the South Twin on the east, and many lesser summits of the range stretched off southward. Hoping to learn the elevation of their peak, they had carried an aneroid barometer on the climb, but all readings were much higher than they knew they should be. Hegg took photographs with an eight-by-ten camera.

The climb was a first. It also was a visit to the heights of the Mount Baker region by a young man who was to distinguish himself later in life with a marvelous photographic record of the Klondike gold rush. E.A. Hegg was twenty-three when he made his South Twin climb. He had been in the Northwest only two years, after moving from Wisconsin to Tacoma to seek his fortune as a commercial photographer. The competition in Tacoma was severe, so he moved north to the communities on Bellingham Bay and opened a studio in New Whatcom. Like most commercial photographers he buttered his bread with studio photography, but his first love was outdoor work. He photographed men in nature extensively, recording the activities of fishermen and loggers in the country around New Whatcom. Then in 1897, the call of the Klondike captured him, as it did many of the young men of New Whatcom; he gathered up his ponderous photographic gear and set off. For four years he recorded the drama of the search for gold from Skagway to Nome, compiling a magnificent and unique record of this historic time, most of which has been preserved.[7]

Yet another party came to climb Mount Baker before the close of the 1891 season. This group came from Seattle and was led by Major E.S. Ingraham, a Seattle school teacher and mountaineer who already had two successful ascents of Mount Rainier to his credit. With Ingraham were G.K.

Coryell, J.V.A. Smith and Fred Calhoun. They came by train to Deming and then hiked over rough road and trail to the mouth of Glacier Creek. From there they struggled for two and half days up Glacier Creek and then Grouse Creek, finally emerging into meadows high on Grouse Ridge, where they set up camp and prepared for their climb. They made one start, only to be turned back by a storm that deposited three feet of new snow on the heights and buckets of rain on the climbers. Finally the weather cleared and they set out.

> Sunday morning dawned upon us clear and cold, the peaks above us glistening in their mantle of virgin snow. We were awake at four o'clock and ready for the ascent by seven. We followed the same course as in the first attempt, in a general way in an easterly direction. After three hours of hard climbing up the glacier, avoiding numerous crevasses by circuitous routes and crossing others on frail snow bridges, we reached the divide between Colfax and the main peak.
>
> From this point the ascent is very abrupt, the first part of the distance continuing along a ridge covered with volcanic ashes several inches deep. The last 500 feet is a wall of seemingly perpendicular appearance. Ordinarily the mountaineer would have to cut steps up this steep wall of ice, but, on account of the new snow which had fallen, we were enabled to make the ascent by means of our alpenstocks alone.[8]

They reached the summit, enjoyed the spectacular view of mountains all around mantled in new snow, then made their way back to camp. Another storm closed in upon them as they reached their tents; it was September and high climbing was over for the year.

It had been quite a year on the mountain. Conditions on Mount Baker and in the surrounding lowlands had been propitious for mountaineering. All over the Northwest many men and a few women were responding to the challenges of the mountains. Most were rank beginners who could not resist the lure of the dominant features of the landscape looming to the east on clear days. Many were climbers content to "conquer" their local giant, but others like Professor Ingraham were the Northwest's first generation of dedicated mountaineers, people who would climb and explore mountains throughout their lives for no other reason than that they loved to do so.

There is no record of other attempts to climb the mountain until July of 1892, when J.M. Edson, one of the party that had made the first ascent of South Twin the previous summer, prepared for an ascent. Edson's party hoped to establish a new route by approaching the mountain along Skyline Divide and Chowder Ridge, unaware of Dorr's unsuccessful attempt. Instead of traveling up Glacier Creek, Edson's group climbed directly up the forested slopes southeast of the confluence of the creek and the North Fork of the Nooksack River, as Dorr had done in 1884. They emerged into alpine meadows at the top of Skyline Divide, and could see that a long ridge walk through open country should take them to a sharp and steep ridge running all the way to the summit. They worked their way out along these ridges, enjoying a magnificent view of Baker's north face. Eventually they came to the pinnacle of unconsolidated rock that had thwarted Dorr and named it "Pumice Stone Pinnacle." It proved too much for them, as it had for Dorr. It fell apart under foot and hand. Steep slopes of snow and ice stretched down to dark crevasses on both sides of the rock. There was no hope of going further that way, so they turned back, disappointed.

These men were mountaineers, not prospectors as Dorr and his friend had been, and were not ready to give up their goal. They turned down Bastille Ridge from Chowder Ridge, losing 4500 feet of elevation as they dropped all the way down to Glacier Creek. With classic understatement one member of the party wrote later: "We then decided to change our position and the next day moved camp to the head of Glacier Creek, a beautiful place for camping, but much lower down than our former camp."[9] On July

The Morovits cabin

31 the party set out to climb by way of Coleman Glacier, ". . . carrying ropes, axes, and our eatables such as fired grouse, stewed huckleberries, biscuits and cold coffee."[10] Seven hours later they were on the summit and were "good and ready for our lunch."[11] The stake left on the summit the previous September by the LaConner party was still there, and they split parts off of it for souvenirs.

> The descent was made by tying ourselves together, turning our faces to the mountain and climbing down backwards for the first thousand feet. The balance of the descent was without any particular incident and we arrived home pretty well worn out though not as badly sunburnt as some of the previous parties.[12]

The summer of 1892 marked the beginning of the career of Mount Baker's first and most unusual mountain guide. His name was Joe Morovits, and he had recently taken up residence in the wilderness meadows at the upper end of Baker Lake. He was building a "ranch" there and prospecting the countryside for gold. Joe was short and stocky, a tough character who became legendary for his feats of strength; over the twenty-seven years that he lived at the foot of Mount Baker's eastern slopes he was called upon many times to assist people who aspired to climb the mountain.

Joe Morovits was born in Wisconsin in 1866 to Bohemian immigrant parents. When he was small, his parents separated and his mother was left to raise seven children. They were poor and life was a struggle. At the age of nine, Joe went to work on a neighbor's farm for a monthly wage of two dollars. He never went to school but learned to read and write from a mining camp bunk-mate when he was twenty-three years old.

As soon as he was able, Joe left home and struck out on his own, working in coal mines in Colorado, Idaho, California, on Vancouver Island and finally in the Blue Canyon Mines at the head of Lake Whatcom, west of Mount Baker. From these mines he moved, at the age of twenty-seven, to the Baker Lake valley—"Morovits country" to a generation of climbers. A letter to Charles Finley Easton describes his life in Baker Lake country:

> I located here two miles west of Baker Lake on the 13th day of October, 1891, built a cabin fit to move into five days later. I lived alone for 27 years. The closest settler was 12 miles down the river. There were no trails before me, not even blazes. I wanted to prospect the mountains for precious metals and settled to stay until I could clean up a few hundred thousand dollars. Singlehanded I drove over 1000 feet of tunnel and shaft work, have washed down thousands of yards of gravel for placer and have built over 40 miles of trail and kept it open all these years. Other settlers came in after me, but left inside of 6 years, as soon as they

Mighty Joe Morovits

proved up on their homesteads and got title to their places. So I have been alone nearly all the time, a Hermit, but a busy one.

I am a jack of all trades. I do iron work and wood work and run my own stamp mill. I put in my own tram, harnessed the water power, took in my own machinery and set it up. I have one piece of iron up there that weighs more than a ton, the mortar.[13]

Joe's feats of strength were legendary—he was the Mount Baker counterpart to the Olympic's Iron Man of the Hoh. He reportedly thought nothing of carrying a hundred-pound pack the thirty-two miles from the general store at Birdsview to his ranch. That was his standard load, and if he had less weight than that after packing his bacon, flour, beans, ammunition and dynamite, he would make up the difference with whiskey.

He accomplished several truly prodigious feats of strength and ingenuity. Two necessary parts of his mining machinery were a die and shoe for his stamp mill. They weighed 2300 pounds. The mill would allow Joe to crush rocks by dropping the "shoe" onto the die; the ore was crushed in water between the two. After crushing, the rock was washed into a mortar box and the gold taken out. The steamboat delivered the shoe and die to Baker City, the present town of Concrete, and Joe set out to move it over the twenty-one miles to his operation. First he hauled it with four horses but the trail became too rough for the team after a few miles. So Joe windlassed, or winched, the mortar from tree to tree the rest of the way—it took two years.[14]

Joe appeared on the Mount Baker climbing scene in 1892. In August six LaConner men asked him to lead them up the mountain. Joe had never been up himself, but thought he could do it without difficulty. The party made their way past Joe's homestead to Rainbow Creek and up to Rainbow Glacier. They climbed the glacier to the rocky ridge known as Landes Cleaver, from which they could look down to the north into what Joe called the "Hot Springs"—the Dorr Fumaroles. Here four of the party decided they were too exhausted to go further. Joe went on with the other two, up the Cleaver to the "Rocks"—The Cockscomb. Faced here with what seemed insurmountable difficulties, the other two LaConner men gave up. Joe describes what happened:

I was packing my rifle, the Lord only knows why. We were all as green as grass when it came to climb a real mountain. I had lots of experience climbing rough mountains in Colorado, hunting, prospecting and trapping, but never climbed a mountain before that was all covered with snow, and perhaps I wouldn't have gone up Mt. Baker that day, after all the other fellows quit, only we got into an argument. Some said that no man could possibly climb up and I said that any man could go up. So just to prove to the crowd that it could be done, I went and found it a thousand times worse than I figured on. The last rise was near the summit and was the worst. It was so steep that I had to cut notches for every step with the rifle, and, coming down, I had to back down and I had to move around many cracks. The weather was perfect, clear as a bell and warm. We had started at five o'clock in the morning and got back to camp about six in the evening. I went direct on the north side. What I call the hot springs is on the north side at the head of Wells Creek, where there is steam coming out in many places, or fumes.[15]

Thus did Joe begin his climbing career. He made the first solo ascent of Mount Baker along the most difficult route yet climbed on the mountain. It was not to be repeated until 1906, when a group of skilled and experienced climbers, members of the Portland-based Mazamas, went that way.

Yet another climb counts in this initial "epidemic of mountaineering." In September a group calling itself the "Streetcar Brigade," all employees of the Fairhaven Streetcar Company, successfully climbed the mountain from the Baker Lake side, though little is known of their exact route.

All of this activity—six parties to the summit in two years—indicates that Mount Baker had become a favorite objective of Northwest adventurers. Access to the area had improved, and people had the leisure and inclination to venture onto the mountain for sport. Successful climbs reported by the press lured other aspirants to the mountain's glaciers. A climb to the summit had become almost commonplace.

5

Gold Mines and Foresters

Wise forest production does not mean the withdrawal of forest resources, whether of wood, water, or grass, from contributing their full share to the welfare of the people, but, on the contrary, gives the assurance of larger and more certain supplies. The fundamental idea of forestry is the perpetuation of forests by use. Forest production is not an end of itself; it is a means to increase and sustain the resources of our country and the industries which depend upon them.

—President Theodore Roosevelt
State of the Union Message, 1901

After the first period of mountaineering in the early 1890s, the pace of climbing on Mount Baker slowed considerably for various reasons. The novelty of climbing the mountain was gone. So many people had been to the summit that it was not the unusual achievement it had been in the early '90s. Further, the economic fortunes of the region, indeed of the entire United States, were at an ebb. Bust followed boom. Banks failed and many were without work. The depression dragged from 1892 to 1898. Men struggling to survive were not interested in climbing for sport. And increased interest in gold in the Mount Baker region and elsewhere diminished the number of climbing efforts. The mid and late '90s saw gold rushes up the North Fork of the Nooksack and, on a far greater scale, to the Klondike. The adventurous rushed off to make their fortunes and were gone for years in which they often had their fill of hardship. Whatever the reason, fewer people ventured onto the slopes of Mount Baker in the late 1890s and early 1900s.

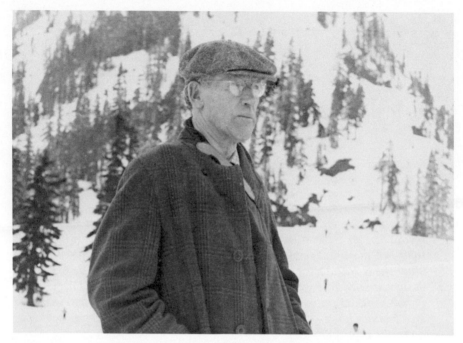

Bert Huntoon, a figure in the history of the region for forty years

The idea for a road across the North Cascades was still alive in 1894, when the road commissioners hired a pair of reputable surveyors to make one last cruise through the Mount Baker country to search for a feasible route. Bert Huntoon and H.M. Wellman were hired for the job. They went up the South Fork of the Nooksack to its headwaters. After several strenuous days they found themselves at "Baker Pass" immediately south of the mountain. Huntoon decided it was time for "a day off," so he and Wellman made a side trip up the glaciers on Baker's south slopes. His terse journal reported:

> At 8 o'clock A.M., we began the ascent of Mt. Baker to obtain what information we could regarding the physical characteristics of the country to be cruised. Our route led us over the big south glacier and winding our way around immense crevasses, we reached the crater at 12:20 pm, after which it took us 1½ hours to climb to the summit one-fourth mile farther.[1]

That was all there was to it for Huntoon—the climb was no big deal. After the climb they went down to Baker River, up Swift Creek to Austin Pass, then out via the North Fork of the Nooksack. They "circumnavigated" the mountain, quite a feat in itself, and returned to New Whatcom with the opinion that no good route for the proposed road existed, which killed any idea of building across the mountains from the headwaters of the Nooksack River.

While Huntoon and Wellman were walking around Mount Baker, a group of climbers was gathering on the slopes of Mount Hood to form a new climbing club called the Mazamas. They were very enthusiastic about climbing throughout the Northwest, and during the summer of 1895 they set out on an ambitious plan to heliograph, or flash messages with mirrors, from Mount Baker in the north to Mount Shasta in the south. Mazamas, all carrying heliographic equipment, would climb Mounts Baker, Rainier, St. Helens, Adams, Hood, Jefferson, Diamond Peak, Three Sisters, Pitt and Shasta on the 9th of July. Weather permitting, they would relay flash messages the entire length of the Cascade Range.

The Mount Baker party, each man with his Merriam pack filled with clothing, appropriate equipment and two double blankets rolled, traveled by train from Portland to Seattle where they caught the steamer *State of Washington* north to New Whatcom. From there they took another train to Sumas, where their packer, William Thompson, was awaiting them with three horses. In addition to their personal gear and food they had "a copper box for records which we expected to leave on the mountain, barometers, cameras, and four carrier pigeons."[2] They set off immediately for the mountain, staying the first night at one of Thompson's cabins, twelve miles along the way, and the second at his last cabin, fifteen miles farther on, beyond Glacier Creek on Thompson Creek.

The men could look up Glacier Creek and see their goal at its head. An argument over how they should approach the mountain developed. Why not go up Glacier Creek? they suggested. But the packer assured them that the shortest and best route to the mountain was up the ridge rising immediately behind his cabin. He claimed to have almost reached the summit by that route, and "practically refused to go the way we had chosen." Thompson prevailed, and next morning the men found themselves struggling through blowdowns on a steep hillside. One Mazama observed:

> Other parties had gone up Glacier Creek canyon which we were leaving to our right. We were strongly advised by the men who had made the trial that way, and by Thompson, that the fatigues and perils being fearful and the possibilities of perishing being considerable, to avoid it. But our way by this time was proving anything but comfortable.[3]

They climbed high on the ridge, cached their food and equipment and went back down to ferry a second load up the next morning. As they descended they were overtaken by darkness and became lost. They had a bad time "passing through ill-smelling damp thickets of devils-clubs" until, with the aid of a full moon, they finally reached Glacier Creek and followed it down to Thompson's cabin. Their expedition had not started well.

The next day they headed back up through the steep brush, reached their cache and proceeded on, eventually climbing out of the woods and into the subalpine parkland on the top of Skyline Divide. They worked their way out along the ridge system only to realize, as had Dorr several years earlier, that they could not reach the summit. Their "guide" had led them astray. "It was now very late in the afternoon. We were stuck up against the very sky at the extreme limit of vegetation, higher than any of the other points around us, with the great, deep canyon of Glacier Creek between us and the opposite side, the way that now looked feasible and the one we first planned on taking."

It seemed unlikely that they would make their heliograph appointment, which was scheduled for next day, but they were determined to be the first Mazamas to climb the mountain. They would have to drop down two thousand feet to Glacier Creek, then make their way to the summit over Coleman Glacier. Descending Bastille Ridge, they encountered further trouble. One fellow "was carrying a 36 inch mercurial barometer strapped to his pack, when in some way it caught and tripped him, falling among some rocks and knotty logs, injuring him internally." They found a fairly level spot on the steep hillside and pitched camp.

All aspiration to climb the mountain was abandoned. For two days they perched there while the injured man recovered enough to travel. They scouted a way out while they waited. Smith Creek drained the west slope of Bastille Ridge and offered the easiest descent. So with their supplies completely exhausted, they descended this creek to where it met Glacier Creek just above its gorge. They camped here and "were fortunate to kill a mess of fish with boulders." Then they commenced their struggle down Glacier Creek, climbing up and down, traversing sidehills, hanging on to shrubbery and devil's club and fighting their way through alder thickets. Much the worse for wear, they eventually reached their guide's cabin at Thompson Creek and ate several huge meals. After a night's rest, they hiked the twenty-seven miles to Sumas in eight hours, finding the trail delightful after the brush they had been through.

The heliograph plan was obviously a failure, and the ill-fated party had no opportunity to use any of the equipment they lugged so laboriously over the countryside. The copper box they were going to leave on the summit went back to Portland with them. The carrier pigeons purchased in Seattle were sent from the mountain with messages but were never heard from. In a letter to Charles Finley Easton in 1912, Martin W. Gorman of the Mazamas added a humorous postscript to his account of the trip. They had such a hard time of it that upon reaching Sumas on the return trip, "one man's clothing was so badly torn that he had to be left out in the woods until the others borrowed some extra garments from the hotel keeper to fix him up for the occasion." It was a tired, sore and frustrated group who boarded the train in Sumas for the trip home.

William Thompson was never again asked to serve as guide for the Mazamas but his failure with them did little to hurt his packing business up the North Fork. While the Mazamas were on the mountain, and for several years thereafter, exploration for gold in the Mount Baker region was increasing. Various "strikes" gave Thompson and other packers all they could do to serve the hundreds, sometimes thousands, of gold-seekers who streamed up the Nooksack valley. Hamilton Wells and Charles Bagley, two local men whose names are now attached to creeks north of the mountain, predicted after a prospecting trip far up the North Fork in 1891 that gold would most surely be found somewhere in the upper Nooksack country. Time was to prove them correct.

Access to the region was becoming increasingly easier. The aborted scheme to cross the mountains with a road resulted in improved road and trail up the river. By the end of 1893 a rough wagon road extended as far as Boulder Creek, a few miles below Glacier. Beyond that the "Cascade State Trail" was improved all the way to Ruth Creek, near the headwaters of the

Packing into the Lone Jack Mine, 1920s

North Fork. Horses could be used on this trail. Scattered settlers were moving into the upper North Fork valley: A.B. Loop to Boulder Creek in 1889, C.C. Cornell and William Thompson to Glacier in 1893.

Many panned and dug for gold in the region. Several found it, most notably Hamilton Wells, Jack Post, Russ Lambert and Lyman G. Valkenberg. Wells, a Union Army drummer boy during the Civil War, settled in New Whatcom in 1887. An avid outdoorsman, he hunted, explored and prospected up the North Fork whenever he could get away. In the early 1890s he found color in Ruth Creek and was convinced that a lode was to be found nearby. His certainty and enthusiasm drew other men into the Ruth Creek area. In 1896 he located what he called the "Silver Tip" lode on Ruth Creek, touching off a flurry of activity in that area. Wells never made any money, but he kept the dream alive crawling all over the hills and mountains north of Mount Baker.

The Lone Jack Mine near Twin Lakes in 1923, shortly before the end of its period of greatest productivity

Jack Post was an old-timer by the time Wells came on the scene. He had come from somewhere during the Fraser River Gold Rush of 1858. For forty years, on and off, he poked around the hills looking for gold, operating out of the thriving little community of Sumas, on the International Boundary just west of the mountain foothills. All those years he found little until, in the mid-1890s, he and two Sumas friends made the biggest strike in the history of the Mount Baker region.

Russ Lambert, the "White Collar Prospector," was in on this strike. He was a Sumas attorney who met Jack Post in town shortly after hanging out his shingle there in 1889. The other Sumas associate was Lyman G. Valkenberg, a logger and homesteader who had lived in the Nooksack Valley since 1882. Post had found gold in Swamp Creek, which flowed from the north into the Nooksack about a mile downstream from its confluence with Ruth Creek. He traced Swamp Creek to its source near Twin Lakes, nestled at five thousand feet between two small mountains. There were also tracings of gold around the lakes. Most significant were boulders of rich quartz in the bed of Silesia Creek, which flowed northeastward just north of the lakes. Post was getting along in years and knew that considerable exploring would be necessary to discover the source of the gold and quartz, so he enlisted the relatively inexperienced Lambert and Valkenberg to assist him. They needed little urging.

The three men had promising claims on Ruth Creek, but these claims assayed toward copper and silver, much less valuable than gold. According to the story, the three were working in the Ruth Creek area in August, 1897, and decided it was time to have another look around Twin Lakes, where prospects seemed more promising. On August 22, they camped by Twin Lakes, at the foot of Winchester Mountain, in Skagway Pass. They divided up the ground to be covered and were off with high hopes at dawn, August 23.

Valkenberg and Lambert found nothing and were stirring their beanpot in camp by the lakes late in the evening when Post came shouting into camp. He had found what he was seeking—a thick quartz outcropping extending across the face of Bear Mountain just north of the lakes which was "fairly bristling" with flecks of gold "as large as peas."[4] Post was sure they had something big, the "mother lode" for which he had been searching for forty years, the dream that keeps every prospector going. We can imagine the three men whooping and hollering and dancing around their fire. Their speculation must have been rampant; undoubtedly a few toasts, if only of coffee, must have been drunk to their prospects. For two days the three set their stakes, marked their claims, and gathered ore samples. Then Lambert set out down Swamp Creek and the Nooksack River to Sumas for supplies and assays.

The men named their find Lone Jack. When Lambert got the assay report he was flabbergasted—"Gold value of ore assayed $10,750 per ton."[5] He had to go to New Whatcom to record the claims, and word spread like wildfire through the community that something big was happening up the river. The assay report struck Sumas like a bolt of lightning—business ground to a halt in the excitement. Lambert secured supplies, packed his ponies and headed out again for Twin Lakes. Many others were not far behind. The greatest gold rush in the history of the Mount Baker region was on.

Local historian Percival Jeffcott describes the aftermath of the strike.

> The three prospectors at once continued their extensive explorations on their five claims in the Post-Lambert Group, but scarcely had they gotten well started, when the first of the vanguard of the now increasing Gold Rush began appearing in the little pocket in the mountains around Twin Lakes, and, pitching their tents, started an intensive search of the vicinity of the big strike for good locations. Almost overnight, the camp mushroomed to near the size of a village; and, visioning the growth of a permanent mining camp, they called it "Union City". Within the course of several weeks, there were 300 to 500 men in the "City" of tents, and before snow fell, as many as 300 claims had been staked in the Lone Jack vicinity. But hundreds of other prospectors were arriving, and fanning out in other parts of the North Fork District, established camps at the mouth of Swamp Creek, called "Trail City"; at the mouth of Ruth Creek, called "Wilson's Townsite"; at the 18 Mile Post on Ruth Creek, known as "Gold City"; and at the present site of Shuksan, which took the name of "Gold Hill", because of its proximity to the big strike on Bear Mountain.[6]

Towns appeared literally overnight at these spots in the upper Nooksack valley. The town of Sumas, home of the three fortunates who started the whole rush, was virtually emptied of men within hours of Lambert's departure. One fellow there was reportedly moving his house when he heard the news of the strike. Leaving the house in the middle of the street, he threw together an outfit and headed for the mines. The paper in New Whatcom reported:

> All hours of the day, may be seen on the streets of the City men starting out in wagons, on horseback, on bicycles and on foot with picks, guns, blankets and provisions, carried in many different ways. Guns, packsaddles, horses, mining location notices, were all in great demand. . . . Everyone seems to be going.[7]

Thousands of feet, horse and human, churned the trail up the Nooksack into a quagmire, and men swarmed over the hills until the snow drove them out in October.

In 1898 they flocked back upriver as soon as snow allowed. Thirty

The Gargett Brothers transporting supplies to their mine early in the twentieth century

cabins were built at Shuksan just west of where Swamp Creek enters the Nooksack. Two stores and a post office also opened. Post, Lambert and Valkenberg sold their mine to a Portland syndicate; this company proceeded rapidly with development. Bridges were built across the Nooksack in several places, and the road was improved so that mining machinery could be taken to the area. The Lone Jack was sold again in 1899, and by 1902 the mine, the aerial tram for transporting ore and the stamp mill for processing it were all operating. The mining industry had finally and truly come to the Mount Baker region. The Lone Jack plant would burn down and be destroyed by avalanches in years to come, but before it died more than a million dollars' worth of gold would be taken from the mine.

Other gold-bearing locations were found. A rich outcropping of gold-bearing quartz was discovered in 1899 about a half mile above the mouth of Wells Creek. A one-mile spur road was extended to it from the State Trail, and the Excelsior Mine eventually went into operation. It was never profitable and closed in 1916. A prospector named Tom Braithwaite, so the story goes, was out hunting goats when he discovered what proved to be the second richest vein in the region. He and a companion were on Red Mountain, now Mount Larrabee, on their hunt, and made a long-range shot at a goat. Upon being hit, the goat tumbled down the mountainside. Reaching their prey they were astounded to see a ledge of quartz flecked with gold. This proved to be the Boundary Red Mountain Gold Mine ledge, just south of the International Boundary. It was to yield some one and a half million dollars' worth of gold.

Prospectors have been combing the hills in numbers around Mount Baker ever since the 1898 Gold Rush. Other finds have been made, but none have paid much. Over five thousand mining claims have been filed in the district, but only the Lone Jack and Boundary Red have yielded profit. Of course, all this activity played a large part in the gradual opening of the region. Roads and bridges were built; thousands of people came in contact with the mountain, if only visually. The way was made easier for the large groups of mountaineers who would come to climb the mountain in the next decade.

Credit should be given to these prospectors for their climbing feats. For them, climbing was only a means to an end, but when we follow their footsteps today through the mountains between Baker and the International Boundary, we marvel at the rough and exposed places they traveled. They were not out for sport so never recorded their climbing exploits. But the cheechacos and sourdoughs, driven by visions of riches and glory, risked their lives countless times in places where modern climbers break out the rope. The story of the prospectors' climbing in the region cannot be told, but it must be acknowledged.

After he and his partners sold the Lone Jack, Jack Post continued his love affair with the Mount Baker region, this time as one of its first "forest guards." Post could thank the newly born conservation movement for his job. Increasing public concern over exploitation of the public domain had led Congress in 1891 to give the president power to establish forest reserves. They would be administered by the General Land Office under the jurisdiction of the Department of the Interior. Before his term expired, President Benjamin Harrison set aside thirteen million acres of such reserves. No means of administering the forests were established; they were simply closed to private exploitation. In 1897, President Grover Cleveland proclaimed another twenty million acres reserved, among them the Washington Forest Reserve, which included the Mount Baker region.

At the outset the status of "reserve" did not provide much protection. No effective mechanism was set up to administer the lands set aside, and few funds were appropriated to hire people to protect the resources. Jack Post went to work as a guard for the General Land Office around 1900. The equipment and instructions he received illustrate the kind of resources he had to work with and the vagueness of his charge. He was given a small axe, a rake, a brushhook, a pitchfork and the following instructions: "take care of the forest, rake up leaves, clean up debris, build cabins, etc., for superior officers."[8]

When the politician's initial outrage subsided (western congressmen were, then as now, often strongly pro-development), Congress acted again

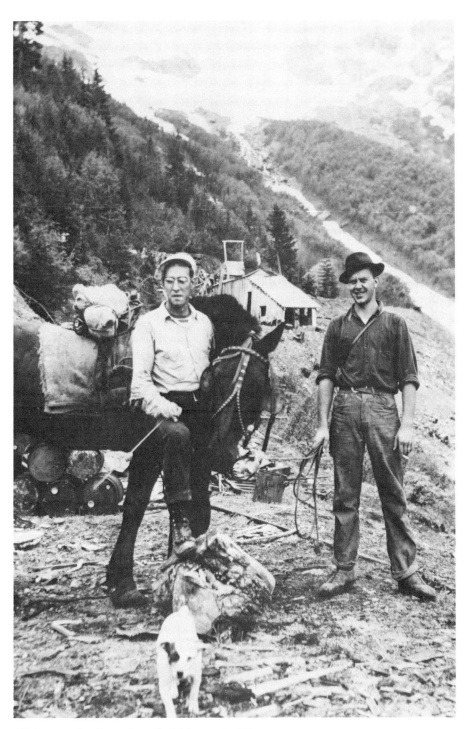

Visitors at the Boundary Red Mountain Mine

to set up management for the reserves. The forests were to be protected from destruction, but timber was to be sold in a controlled way. A principle of use and a system of supervision and administration were set up under the Department of the Interior. The program was, however, one of custody rather than real management and use.

In 1898 a young forester named Gifford Pinchot became Chief of the Division of Forestry in the Department of Agriculture. While his group had no control over the forest reserves, he developed an effective organization within his limited jurisdiction and worked to transfer the reserves from the Department of the Interior to Agriculture. Pinchot argued that trees were a renewable agricultural crop and logically were the concern of the Department of Agriculture; in 1905 his view prevailed. President Theodore Roosevelt, who supported Pinchot's ideas, pushed the Transfer Act of 1905 through Congress. Pinchot's division became the United States Forest Service, and a new character appeared on the scene—the forest ranger.

The earliest rangers in the Mount Baker region were not trained foresters like Pinchot, but local men who knew the country and possessed the skills needed to establish a lawful presence on the land. Jack Post was one such man. John W. Barber, who was appointed to the North Fork Nooksack District of the Washington Forest Reserve in 1899, was another. A brief article about him appeared in the New Whatcom paper at the time.

> Barber is an old pioneer in the mountains and is familiar with the area to which he has been assigned, having lived there since 1893. He has worked as a woodsman, pioneer, hunter and trapper and is known all over as Daniel Boone of Blaine.
>
> Barber will build cabins at Glacier Creek and at the twenty milepost on the Cascade State Road, at both of which places he expects to keep a headquarters. He is very much alive to the necessity of keeping fires out of our National Forests.[9]

Early rangers like Post, Barber, O.G. Armstrong, Carl Bell and Joe Ridley had to be jacks-of-all-trades, able to work with axe, saw, hammer, transit, pack animal, mason's trowel and various mechanical gadgets. It was no easy task to qualify for the job, as C.C. McGuire notes in his memoirs.

> As memory serves me, the following tests were given: (1) From the foliage, identify ten species of trees grown on the Mt. Baker— give common and technical names—if you can spell the latter, more power to you. (2) Fall a tree ten or more inches in diameter with an axe. In giving this test a stake was driven in the ground about twenty feet from the tree. The victim was allowed to select the point where the stake was driven. All he had to do then was to fall the tree so that it would drive the stake further into the

ground. His skill was determined by the nearness of the tree bole to the stake. Only three candidates out of sixteen survived that test, one man actually driving the stake. Most trees went wide of the mark with some trees falling in the opposite direction. (3) Figure magnetic declinations on the four quadrants of the compass. . . . (4) Run and pace a triangle; prepare the field notes and compute the acreage. (5) Demonstrate your ability to use a seven-foot cross-cut saw. (6) Tell the boss what ingredients and how much each you would use in preparing a batch of biscuits. (7) Build and put out a campfire. . . . (8) Pack a horse. This was a toughy. . . . Not only was your skill tested but you worked against time. Many would-be rangers fell by the wayside on this test. One bewildered candidate got the pack saddle on backwards with the britchen over the horse's head and used the breast strap for a double hitch.[10]

Men who passed the test worked on patrolling their territory, building trails, bridges and cabins. The first Forest Service headquarters in the Mount Baker region was built on Gallop Creek, in the town of Glacier, in 1907. A four-room dwelling with no plumbing or other conveniences, a shop, warehouse and barn made up the station. Rangers Joe Ridley and Carl Bell built the Deming Ranger Station in 1908 at the National Forest boundary. Bell lived there with his wife and three sons, keeping the station open for hikers once a trail was built up the river in 1909.

Life was often tough for these early rangers, but that was one reason they signed on. They enjoyed the challenges of travel in rugged country, of exploring and protecting their vast domain. In 1908 the Washington Forest Reserve was divided up into four "national forests": the Chelan, Wenatchee, Snoqualmie and Washington National Forests. The latter, which included the Mount Baker region (the name was changed to Mount Baker National Forest in 1926), in turn was divided into four districts. Parts of the Mount Baker region fell into the North Fork Nooksack District No. 1 (later the Glacier Ranger District) and the Baker River District No. 2. The North Fork District encompassed 225,860 acres.

Patrolling such a vast territory for fires and various illegal activities often took rangers into the field for weeks or even months. They often transferred between districts as work required more men here or there. McGuire spent three years bounding around the Baker River and Nooksack districts; his feelings about finally becoming a "district" ranger at Glacier in 1913 tell much about the life these men led.

I had a wife and two children and began to wonder if in this job of Forest Ranger I would ever get to live with them, but that spring Ranger Jones quit and I got the Glacier Station. Here, for the first

Early loggers among the big trees

time, I felt that I definitely had a job, could have my family with me and need not wonder where I would land next. The Ranger's house was a four-room affair, each room ten by twelve, no plumbing or built-in "folderols." A fireplace was built in the center of the building but at its best it made a good smoke house, and at its worst, well, we just moved outside until the fire went out. My first Sunday I started tearing it out . . . . I laid up the brick for the chimney and my wife carried the hod. We lived in this shack for 6 years. The house also served as an office and the dining room table was my desk . . . . [11]

The United States Forest Service would from this time on manage and administer the Mount Baker region. They attempted to mediate conflicting demands for use of the area's resources and determined in large measure how men and women would change the environment of the mountain and its surroundings.

There was still more Federal Government involvement in the area. By executive order of May 10, 1899, Baker Lake and surrounding lands within one-half mile of the shore were reserved for the use of the United States Commissioner of Fish and Fisheries for a "fish cultural station." Construction of a hatchery was begun, and a salmon production program began in 1907. This installation included improvement of the trail and ultimately the construction of a road into the Baker Lake area. An ill-fated facility, its operation was interrupted three times, twice by fire and once by a crushing snowpack. The hatchery operated until 1940, when the land and improvements were transferred from the Bureau of Fisheries to the Forest Service.

A few people were climbing Mount Baker while the politicians and bureaucrats were deciding how the area should be managed and the forest rangers were making their first tentative efforts. Joe Morovits, untouched by activities in Washington, D.C. and the gold rushes to the North Fork and the Klondike (he knew of the latter, for his brother, who homesteaded near him for two years, headed north with the argonauts in 1897), continued his prospecting and climbing. He climbed Boulder Ridge in July, 1894, and traveled the same route again in each of the next two summers. His brother, newly arrived in 1895, joined him for the 1895 climb. He made his fifth ascent in 1900, leading a party of eight up Boulder Ridge. Their climb was uneventful but significant because it introduced John A. Lee to the mountain. Lee, the principal of New Whatcom High School, would soon move to Portland to practice law. He would become a member and leader of the Mazamas, and would return to Mount Baker many times. Also in the party were a forest ranger and two instructors from Bellingham Normal School, a college which would pour a veritable stream of eager young climbers onto the mountain for various adventures and misadventures in years to come.

The mountain was climbed again in 1903 by one of the most experienced Northwest climbers of the day—C.E. Rusk. Rusk came to the mountain twice, succeeding on his second try. His wife was with him the first time. They made a long hike from Baker City to timberline on Boulder Ridge, only to be frustrated there by a storm. On his second attempt a few weeks later he was joined by George Cantwell, a photographer, and W.A. Alexander. They ascended Boulder Ridge, Cantwell and Rusk finishing the route differently than anyone else had. Instead of angling leftward from the top of the ridge and finishing the climb on Boulder Glacier, they went up and slightly to the right. This required delicate negotiation of unstable rock just below the summit of Grant Peak. The rock took a long time to climb. They were late arriving on the summit and were benighted on Boulder Ridge. They descended in the dark without incident and thoroughly enjoyed themselves, according to Rusk's account of the climb.[12]

6

Mountaineering Clubs
Open Mount Baker

A trip into the Mount Baker country every season for a couple of weeks or more, will most assuredly improve the health in every way. Besides, your disposition will be greatly improved, and that grouch you had against everyone you met, will disappear into thin air, just like the clouds disappear from the dome of Mount Baker in the early morning at sunrise. Take a "hike" up on the eastern slopes of the mountain some morning and view the glorious sunrise, and you will feel better toward all mankind ever afterwards.

—L.R. Markley, M.D., 1913

A group of people came together in Oregon in 1884 and formed the Pacific Northwest's first mountaineering group, the Oregon Alpine Club. The idea for the club undoubtedly came from the only other such club in the United States at the time, the Appalachian Mountain Club, the inspiration for which had come in turn from the world's first mountaineering organization, the Alpine Club formed by a group of Englishmen in 1857. Following the English lead, many such clubs had formed throughout Europe in the 1860s and 1870s. They provided the opportunity for like-minded people to join together in pursuit of adventure in the mountains.

These clubs often gathered to socialize as well as hike and climb, and before many years passed, an element in the Oregon Alpine Club began to grumble about the direction the club was

"THE CORNICE" — BRIM OF THE FLAT-TOPPED SUMMIT

The Mountaineers probing for a crevasse, 1908

taking. There were, they thought, too many "elevator riding" mountaineers "bent on submerging the original character of the Club."[1] So, in 1894, the "true mountaineers" of the Oregon Alpine Club formed a new group which would be "composed exclusively of *real* mountain climbers."[2] To make sure that only serious mountaineers would found the group, "this club was to be voted into being upon the icy summit of majestic Mount Hood."[3] This was accomplished, a Chinook Indian motto "Nesika Klatawa Sahale" or "We Climb High!" was adopted and the group took the name Mazamas, or "mountain goats." It was this group that tried the ambitious heliographics mentioned earlier.

The Mazamas instituted a program of annual outings, beginning with a trip to Crater Lake in 1896. These were large undertakings. Many people went, some to climb, some not, but all to enjoy the mountains. After the Crater Lake trip the group established a habit of visiting the Northwest's large volcanoes, Mounts Rainier, Adams, Jefferson, Hood, Adams, the Three Sisters and Shasta in the next decade. They chose Mount Baker as the object of their annual outing in 1906.

Preparations began well in advance of the trip; the group would be a large one requiring a considerable string of pack horses to carry their equipment and food to a base camp. They wanted to go to the northern side of the

LAST CLIMB

Mazama hotshots scaled the summit while their companions slept in camp below, 1906.

mountain, which had not been explored extensively. To do this a trail for their pack train would have to be built. Correspondence flew back and forth between club officers and the Washington Forest Reserve office in Sumas. The Forest Service eventually agreed to construct a trail to a point where the climbers could reach the northern and eastern slopes of the mountain. The rangers needed a trail into the area anyway because they were seeking a way to get from Nooksack River valley to the Baker River valley. It was a long trip around the foothills west of Mount Baker. A trail had already been built up the Baker River valley and up Swift Creek for several miles, and the foresters thought they could connect the new trail with this one. This would greatly help the rangers cover their large territories.

During the last week of July no less than 118 Mazamas gathered at Sumas. Packers and horses were waiting for them with their supplies. The size of the task is revealed by the number of eggs packed and ready to go—two hundred dozen! The caravan set off up the road to Glacier and beyond to where the new trail left the river and climbed south toward Mount Baker. The trail went up Wells Creek then over the northern shoulder of Slate Mountain and down to a group of subalpine lakes nestled below the western cliffs of Table Mountain. Their base camp, named Camp Sholes in honor of their president, was pitched at the edge of Hayes Lake. The lakes were collectively known as Galena Lakes to the prospectors who had poked into the hills around them. But the Mazamas called them Chain Lakes; ultimately the compromise name of Galena Chain Lakes became their official designation.

Three scouting parties went out to locate a route to Mount Baker's summit. A ridge, which the group named Ptarmigan Ridge, extends from Table Mountain some four miles to the northeast base of Mount Baker, where the scouting parties could step onto the glaciers that gradually rise to the summit. One party turned southeastward onto Park Glacier but could not go far because of crevasses. The other climbed high on the peak, eventually reaching Pumice Stone Pinnacle. They could not get around this obstruction but thought that with more people and time they might be able to find a way over or around it. The scouts returned to Camp Sholes confident that, with the skilled leadership of people like Asahel Curtis and other veterans of Mounts Hood, Adams and Rainier, a way up would certainly be found.

While the scouting parties were out, the rest of the group enjoyed themselves at Camp Sholes. A high cliff loomed above their tents, forming the western edge of Table Mountain. The group made various short but exciting climbs on this cliff, which they called Mazama Dome. They went swimming in the third lake in the chain, which they called Natatorium Lake—the women swam in the forenoon, the men in the afternoon. Most of the group were city dwellers, and they marveled at the perseverance of a pair of gold miners, Arbuthnot and Davis, who had tunneled through a big rocky ridge in the 1890s and lowered the fourth lake nine feet to reach a vein of ore. The weather was good, though mosquitoes were abundant, and they all took their meals together around a large table built by their enterprising cooks.

On August 4, pack horses were loaded and thirty-five climbers set out to climb the mountain. They went out Ptarmigan Ridge and passed a sharp pinnacle, which they named Coleman Peak in honor of Edmund T. Coleman. They needed fuel for cooking fires, so they made camp near the last available firewood. They named the place Camp Kiser, in honor of the outing's leader, F.H. Kiser of Portland.

The weather remained clear, so early next morning the party roped up and set off on their climb. They figured they had about four and a half miles to travel to the top, which seemed reasonable. Crossing Rainbow Glacier they found the traveling very slow because of extensive crevasses. They then climbed a ridge of rotten rock. To their right was another glacial expanse, which they named in honor of their organization.

One member of the party, Henry Landes, was Washington State Geologist and a geology professor at the University of Washington. Looking north down onto Mazama Glacier, he spotted the Dorr Fumaroles and, with his brother, gave up the climb and descended to explore them. They found an area completely surrounded by glacier, some two acres in extent and actively steaming. Hot springs abounded, forming steaming streams that ran under glacier ice. The air was acrid with sulphur.

The other thirty-three continued upward, reaching Pumice Stone Pinnacle at three o'clock. It is doubtful whether they knew that previous parties had visited this spot, though from a different direction, and had been stopped by the formation. But they would not have been discouraged, being true mountaineers, accustomed to overcoming obstacles judged unclimbable by earlier generations. While most of the group tiredly sat on what they called the "Hill of Patience," looking beyond the rotten pinnacle to the summit so tantalizingly close, nine of the best climbers sought a way around the obstacle. Huge crevasses blocked them, but they thought they could surpass them with time. But the hour was late. When, after five hours' work, they had not overcome the problems, they gave up the attempt, and the whole party returned to Camp Kiser.

Next morning, before most of the party was awake, Kiser and five others walked quietly out of camp. Only the strongest climbers were included, and they left before others who might wish to go were awake—which was to cause bitter feelings later. They retraced their track of the previous day and soon were at work on a route around the pinnacle. The party included Kiser, Curtis, Lee (who had climbed the mountain six years earlier with Joe Morovits), Rodney Glisan and two others. These six traversed below the pinnacle, eventually surmounting steep slopes and the bergshrund, and climbed onto the summit plateau. To their surprise, they found a copy of the Mazama prospectus on the summit, left there the previous day, August 6, by C.C. Cornell, one of the early settlers of Glacier,

Major Pioneering Club Outings

American Border Pk ▲
✖ Boundary Red Mine
Mt. Larrabee ▲
Silesia Creek
Tomyhoi Peak ▲
Twin Lakes
Swamp Creek
✖ Lone Jack Mine
Church Mtn. ▲
Goat Mtn. ▲
Granite Mtn. ▲
Ruth Creek
North Fork Nooksack River
Canyon Creek
✖ Excelsior Mine
Mt. Sefrit ▲
Hannegan Pass
Chilliwack River
GLACIER
Wells Creek
Mt. Herman ▲
Ski Area
Ruth Mtn. ▲
Skyline Divide
Glacier Creek
Table Mtn. ▲
Icy Peak ▲
Hadley Peak ▲
Mt. Shuksan ▲
Grouse Butte ▲
Coleman Pinnacle
Baker River
Coleman Glacier
Swift Creek
Mt. Baker ▲
Shuksan Creek
Easton Glacier
Middle Fork Nooksack River
Morovits Ranch
Boulder Creek
Baker Lake
Twin Sisters Mtn. ▲
Loomis Mtn. ▲
Sulphur Creek
Sandy Creek
Koma Kulshan Ranger Station
Dock Butte ▲
Diobsud Buttes
South Fork Nooksack River
Goat Mtn. ▲
Baker River
Diobsud Creek
CONCRETE
Jackman Creek
Skagit River

------- 1906 Mazamas
············· 1908 Mountaineers
—·—·—· 1909 Mazamas

95

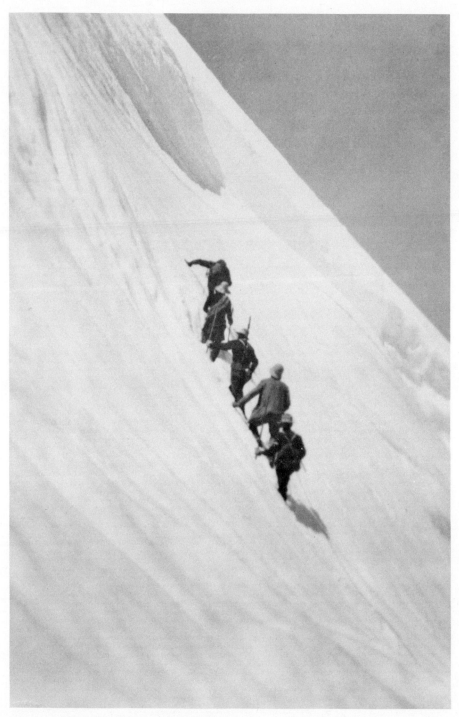

"The six immortals" on successful climb of upper Park Glacier. Asahel Curtis, the sixth "immortal," is behind the camera.

and a Mr. Stewart of Blaine. These two had traversed across Park Glacier while the Mazama group was climbing toward the pinnacle. They had stayed high, avoiding the crevasses lower on the glacier, and had finished the climb as from Boulder Ridge.

Kiser and his group were elated nonetheless, for they thought they had pioneered a new route on the mountain. They had indeed made a difficult climb, but Joe Morovits had preceded them by fourteen years, hacking steps with his rifle butt. They placed a Mazama summit register on the highest point, climbed back down, and returned to Camp Sholes.

Curtis, Lee and Glisan had climbed the big one but were ready for more. As Curtis traveled back and forth along Ptarmigan Ridge, he eyed Mount Shuksan's bulky form to the east. It looked like a tough climb. Hung with glaciers, its summit a sharp spire, its western walls looked steep and difficult. As far as Curtis knew, no one had yet reached the summit, so he decided to try for the first ascent.

Curtis was thirty-two years old. In 1887 he and his brother Edward had moved with their family to Seattle. When their father died in the early 1890s, both young men became professional photographers. Edward specialized in photographic studies of Native Americans, which were to make him famous; Asahel embarked on a career as a commercial photographer. He was already known for his excellent mountain photography and would go on to pioneer the use of photography as a tool for the promotion of economic development of the State of Washington and the City of Seattle. For the moment, however, he was focused on another goal—Mount Shuksan.

Joined by another eager young climber, Montelius Price, Curtis set off from Camp Sholes. The two men crossed the broad summit of Table Mountain, then walked across Austin Pass and along the ridge known as Shuksan Arm. When viewed from Table Mountain, this seemed a feasible approach, for it looked like the ridge joined the main body of Shuksan just west of the summit. But the ridge proved to be very difficult traveling, and they were forced into a deep gorge. Curtis and Price kept at it, but after fourteen hours they found themselves, late in the day, looking from a crag "almost directly beneath the main summit, but separated from it by great glaciers deep with crevasses. A way might be found through this maze, but it would require days of work."[4] They gave up the attempt and made the long trip back to camp.

After a day of rest Curtis and Price again set off for Mount Shuksan. This time they descended into the valley of Swift Creek and climbed what they called Shuksan Ridge, from which they could look across another valley at a cascading glacier. They were undoubtedly near Lake Ann, though they do not mention a lake in their narrative, looking across the valley of Shuksan Creek at what would be named Upper Curtis Glacier. They descended again, going southward along the base of the mountain's western wall. Climbing over talus and moraine, they followed a goat trail up slabby rock and gully to timberline part way up the ridge. As the day ended, the place felt eerie.

> Sunset found us on a spur at timberline, the lower world lost in the haze from forest fires. The ridges of the mountain disappeared in the smoke below and we felt that our camp was suspended above the world. Across the valley the rounded shoulder of a foothill was visible while outlined in the west was the mighty dome of Baker like some fairy creation in the heavens, rather than a mountain of the earth. Its foothills were gone and the haze softened the icy slopes behind which the sun was setting.[5]

After a cold night, they continued up rock and snow until "before us stretched the great snowfields that cover the main plateau."[6] Sulphide Glacier lay before them. To the east rose lesser pinnacles, with the North Cascades jiggling the horizon beyond. The glacier rose gradually to the summit spire, and soon they were climbing its rock. The climbing was easier than it looked, and before long they were on the summit.

There was no sign that anyone had been there before them—no cairn, tobacco can or any of the usual marks men leave on mountain tops. They built a cairn, took photographs, basked in the warm sun and drank in the view. Baker loomed before them to the west. The eastern horizon was a jumble of hundreds of peaks, enough to challenge them for a lifetime. Joe Morovits would later claim that he had made the first ascent of Shuksan, and he may well have. It rose virtually from his back doorstep, and his adventures on Mount Baker clearly testify to his capability. His story was that he climbed the peak while prospecting and, not thinking it a very significant achievement, had not bothered to leave a mark. Joe may have made the first ascent, but he couldn't prove his claim, so Curtis and Price are credited with the achievement.

John A. Lee and Rodney Glisan meanwhile decided they wanted to climb Baker again. Lee, a former president of the Mazamas, once a school teacher in Bellingham and then a Portland attorney, had climbed Boulder Glacier years before with Morovits and may have wished to show his friend Glisan the sights farther east on the mountain. Glisan was also a Portland attorney and avid amateur photographer (he would amass 147 photo albums). The two men, accompanied by a Professor Gleason, set off out Ptarmigan Ridge for another attempt on Koma Kulshan.

As the trio traversed around Coleman Peak, they dropped down into the gorge of Rainbow Creek rather than continue out the ridge to the glaciers, as they had done previously. Crossing the creek, they struggled up the steep southern wall of the gorge, managing only to make it out of the gorge and onto the ridge beyond by nightfall. They had dropped three thousand feet before winning back half of it in their subsequent ascent.

Asahel Curtis (left) *and Montelius Price* (below) *on the summit of Mount Shuksan, 1906*

Next morning they descended the ridge, which was in fact a wide plateau—known today as Lava Divide—looking for a way to get onto Mount Baker proper. Their problem was that between them and their route lay another great gorge, the bottom of which was the much crevassed Park Glacier. They could get to this glacier, but it was overhung by massive ice walls above a band of cliffs which calved thundering avalanches onto Park Glacier's lower surface.

The three men continued down Lava Divide, losing elevation until they came to a meadow on the eastern edge, where a waterfall dropped down to Park Creek below the snout of the glacier. Professor Gleason looked over the edge. He noted that a thousand-foot descent would be necessary, followed by an eight-thousand-foot climb to the summit, and decided he would stay in the luxurious meadow.

Glisan and Lee, young, ambitious and brash, decided they were up to the task and left everything but light lunch, rope and ice axe with the professor (coats and sweaters as well). They dropped off the ridge down to the creek, crossed it and started upward. By noon they had made remarkable progress, gaining five thousand feet, and had stopped for lunch on Boulder Cleaver. Finding to their dismay that they had left most of their lunch behind, they ate what they had and turned upward again.

The ground was familiar to Lee, but above the cleaver the glacier was heavily crevassed. Travel was extremely slow. It took them almost seven hours to negotiate the upper part of the mountain. At 6:45 they signed the recently placed Mazama summit register. Confident of a quick descent they turned immediately downward, but all did not go as well as anticipated.

> . . .we soon had difficulty in retracing our path, which we must do, or otherwise be pocketed in the interlacing crevasses. Lee let his alpenstock slip, and it disappeared in the gloom. Fortunately it was recovered, but valuable time passed, and soon all trace of our track was lost and we were obliged to stop where we were and wait for the moon to aid us. It was somewhat wearisome waiting, having no shelter on the glacier and no rocks to rest on. We crept below the surface of the glacier into a shallow crevasse, but the night-breeze followed us, and as we had no coats or sweaters to keep us warm, we had to act like King George and his men, go down hill a little way and then up again.[7]

Fortunately, the night was rather mild and they survived. "After the lapse of several centuries Dawn appeared"[8] wrote Glisan afterward, and they wasted no time on the downward track.

Once on Boulder Cleaver, Glisan and Lee decided they could save themselves a lot of trouble by traversing Park Glacier above Park Cliffs, then simply drop down to Lava Divide. This was a good idea, but they were

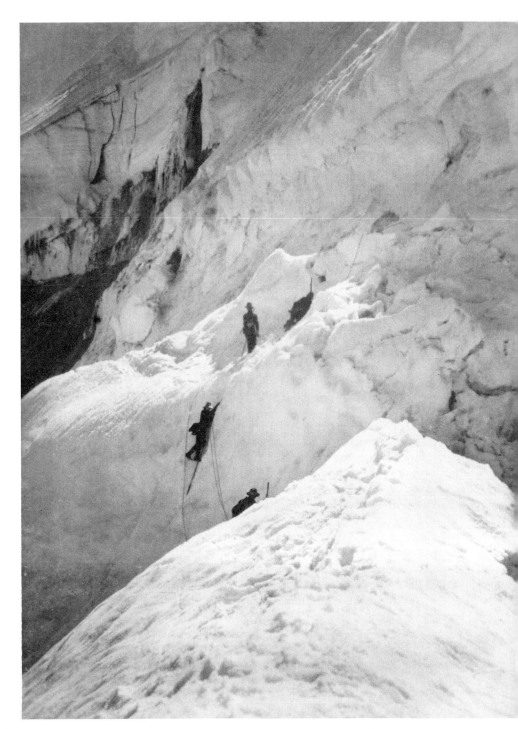

Climbers solving a route-finding problem on a glacier high on the mountain

turned back by crevasses and forced to return to their original route. As they stood again on Boulder Cleaver, they could see their friend Gleason across the divide, not so far away, and even hear his shouts. Exhausted and hungry, they dropped once more down to Park Creek. Food and rest, they thought, would soon be theirs.

The warm weather, which had favored them overnight, now frustrated them. Park Creek was a roaring torrent, fed by rapid snowmelt and glacial runoff. They could not cross and were forced to follow the stream up to where it emerges from beneath the glacier. Using the snout of ice as a bridge, they reached the north side of the stream, then struggled for hours on the north canyon wall. Finally, thirteen hours after they had exchanged shouts with Professor Gleason, they stumbled, in the dark, into their camp. Glisan and Lee had been on their feet for forty hours. They had eaten very little, traveled many miles, and gained and lost more than eleven thousand feet of elevation. What they had thought would be a quick run up the mountain had turned into an epic.

Their work was not over yet; next morning they had to travel twelve rugged miles back to Camp Sholes, only to find horses packed and everyone ready to go home. With barely a rest, the climbers joined the long march back to Sumas for the train ride home to Portland. Glisan and Lee were the first to bivouac near the summit since Coleman and Bennett had done so forty years before. They exhibited tremendous endurance on their four-day trip. They had made the most of the Mazama outing, making two strenuous multi-day ascents of the peak. Most of the Mazamas, to their irritation, had not made it to the summit at all.

The Mazama outing was the beginning of a new mountaineering era in Mount Baker's history. The group was by far the largest ever to travel into the region for recreation. The outing brought together men and women with climbing experience and ambition, and increasing numbers of such people would try to climb ever more difficult routes on the peak. A new access route was opened to the mountain, and mountaineers thoroughly explored areas visited in the past only briefly by Indians and prospectors. The trip was highly successful from both a recreational and mountaineering standpoint, and their descriptions of fun and adventure, published in various magazines, motivated many others to come to Mount Baker. The Mazamas would return in 1909 and many times thereafter.

The other major Northwest climbing club—The Mountaineers from Seattle—came to Mount Baker in 1908. The Mountaineers were formed when a group of Seattle Mazamas decided in 1906 to establish its own group. The Mountaineers grew rapidly and adopted the approach of the Mazamas, sponsoring an annual outing as the highlight of the year. The 1908 outing was to Mount Baker. The group was not quite as large as the Mazama group had been—only fifty people. Asahel Curtis, L.A. Nelson and John Best, Jr., the outing's three leaders, had made a reconnaissance into

The Mountaineers near the summit, 1908

the Baker Lake region early in the summer—the eastern side would be the group's object. They spent ten days locating the trail that would have to be built to timberline, selecting the campsites and arranging for pack animals. They probably enlisted Joe Morovits' assistance. They would need a good trail, for they would bring thirty-two pack animals and a cow, which would be slaughtered at base camp to provide fresh meat.

Most of the group arrived by train at Baker (Concrete) on July 18. They immediately set out up the trail toward Baker Lake and two miles along found their advance party. Camp was all set up for them, the fire was roaring, dinner was waiting. Next morning, aroused by a bugle call, they set off on the twelve-mile hike to Baker Lake. From the lake they traveled Joe Morovits' trail, then over the seven miles of new trail their group had built, until they reached base camp near timberline. Conditions were not ideal

The Mountaineers descending eastern slope of Mount Baker, 1908

there, so they continued another mile before they finally estabished base camp—Mountaineer Camp. The unfortunate cow was duly slaughtered, the horses tethered; the group settled down to enjoy themselves.

This group was not pioneering new ground like the Mazamas had two years before. They were at the base of Boulder Ridge, below Boulder Glacier. Joe Morovits had hiked and climbed all over the area. Various parties had climbed this side, many led by Joe. The greatest contribution of The Mountaineers' outing was the trail that it opened up to Boulder Ridge. All previous parties had struggled with the steep and heavily forested approach. After The Mountaineers, even cows could make the trip.

Camp established, the group enjoyed a mountaineering class on the snow. Curtis and the other experienced climbers showed the novices rudiments of climbing technique. The next day forty-two members of the party climbed to six thousand feet and explored the glaciers. They got a feel for the terrain and surveyed the difficulties of the climbing route to the summit. They would try for the top the following day.

An early morning start was planned, but a storm hit the mountain. For two days wind and rain buffeted the camp. Clouds draped themselves over the glaciers. Climbing was out of the question. Campfire and camaraderie were the order of the day until on the third day the weather cleared. Much to the surprise of the comfortable Mountaineers, a party of cold, wet, bedraggled but relieved climbers came down Boulder Ridge into their camp. Led by Charles Finley Easton, this group had traversed the mountain and spent three uncomfortable nights near the summit in the storm.

The "official" Mountaineers' climb was made up Boulder Ridge and Boulder Glacier. Thirty-nine people made the straightforward and uneventful ascent. Several large crevasses near the summit required care, but everyone negotiated them successfully. The outing was judged by all involved to be a great success, a "conquest" according to the trip's historian, Lulie Nettleton, who used military metaphor throughout her description of the outing.[9]

Charles Finley Easton

Climbers cross the crevasse in which two days earlier the Easton-Sprague party spent the night while waiting out a storm.

The real story of the "mountaineer" period on the mountain was that of Easton and his rain-soaked companions. Charles Finley Easton had been with the Mazama party in 1906 but had failed to make the summit. In 1908 he planned a climb to coincide with The Mountaineers' visit. He and his companions would make a leisurely approach up Glacier Creek and Grouse Ridge, then climb to the summit and spend a couple of days camped there. He hoped to be there when Curtis and his group arrived, and would greet them on "his" mountain. By 1908 Easton was passionately interested in all of Baker's facets. He was not its official historian yet, and would not be until the formation of the Mount Baker Club in 1911, but he had begun his systematic and thorough study of Koma Kulshan.

While The Mountaineers' caravan made its way to base camp, Easton and three other climbers came up the mountain from the west. All went well until they neared the summit, where a strong wind began to blow.

Clouds built up rapidly, and the four suddenly found themselves in a dangerous situation. They were wet with perspiration after climbing in the hot sun and were rapidly chilled by the damp, cold wind. Two of the party were particularly affected, both physically and emotionally, by the ordeal.

Fortunately, they were near a cleaver of rock just below the summit, and there was a moat between the rock and glacier. Moats form in summer, when rock absorbs the warmth of the sun and melts any snow in contact with it. Easton and another strong climber descended into this moat and dug a snow cave into which the whole party crowded. Down in the moat they were out of the howling wind and in relative comfort could enlarge their cave. Eventually they got their stove going, melted snow for water and even dried some of their clothing. The four passed a fairly comfortable night in the cave.

The next morning conditions seemed to have improved a little. They climbed upward, reaching the summit and emerging into cold and windy sunlight. They were in the midst of a wind-tossed sea of cloud. Only the summits of Mount Shuksan to the east and Mount Rainier far to the south were visible. The biting cold soon drove them off the summit and back to their cave, where they debated the next move.

A return trip down the way they had come did not appeal to them. Several very steep and broken sections of glacier had been negotiated, and Easton was not certain that he could retrace his way back down the glacier in the storm. Conditions were again terrible, cloud and snow so thick that it was difficult, sometimes impossible, to distinguish snow from air. They easily could have walked off the edge of a crevasse or steep wall without seeing it. An alternative was to complete the traverse and go down the eastern side, where The Mountaineers' camp was located. Though severe conditions might prevail there, too, Easton reasoned that he and his companions might soon meet The Mountaineers climbing up. Easton also knew that if they could reach Boulder Cleaver, which extended high on Baker's eastern side, they could follow it down. The plan was a gamble, but the odds seemed better to the east than on the broad glacial expanses to the west and south.

Leaving the ice cave after a second night, they had to traverse northeast and then descend. The steep slopes of the crater forced them upward before they could go down. Slowly they groped their way downward, cautiously negotiating the bergshrund at the top of Boulder Glacier and the initially steep upper slopes. Soon they found themselves in a heavily crevassed section of the glacier. Visibility remained near zero as they spent the remaining daylight hours slowly threading their way among crevasses. As night again fell they were blocked from further downward progress by an immense crevasse. The dream of a warm campfire at treeline faded as they faced another cold bivouac.

Casting about for some way to get out of the wind, they found a crevasse in which a large block of snow was wedged, providing a level platform

MT. BAKER VIEWS—MAZAMA SERIES—THE SUMMIT JUST ABOVE.

Mazamas taking a break below the summit, 1909

out of the storm. After gathering flat stones from a nearby cleaver and laying them on the snow platform, the whole party descended into the crevasse for the night. Easton describes the trials that followed.

> One of the most disagreeable features of this night's lodging in cold storage was the chilly current of air that rose from the unknown depths of the crevasse like the draft of some immense flue . . . . That night in the crevasse every few minutes the ice would snap with a sharp, short twing accompanied by a perceptible movement, never more than the smallest fraction of an inch but an unmistakeable slipping, a movement which would probably not be noticed from the surface above. The whole field of ice seemed to be on the move . . . . In our refrigeration . . . we could hear the cracking of the glaciers for miles and miles through on the opposite side of the mountain, and faint rumblings, which may have been due to the grinding of the ice upon the rocks or it may have come from the bowels of the earth where Pluto is working up another volcanic eruption.[10]

As dawn approached, the weather improved and warmed markedly. They crawled out of their chilly refuge to see Boulder Cleaver not far away. Easton had made his traverse, the first on record, though all had not gone as planned. The four went down the ridge and before long were luxuriating in dry clothing, with hot tea, a roaring fire and The Mountaineers.

The Mazamas decided to come back to Mount Baker for their annual outing in 1909. This time they would visit the side opposite their previous explorations, and they hoped it would provide opportunity for more members of the group to climb to the summit than had the outing three years before. Once again they contacted the Forest Service for assistance with access and received plenty of help. There was a rough wagon road a short distance along the Middle Fork of the Nooksack River and a trail five miles to the Washington National Forest boundary. The Forest Service had built their Deming Ranger Station near the boundary in 1908. To reach the southern slopes of Mount Baker, it would be necessary to extend the trail eleven miles beyond the ranger station to timberline.

Forest Supervisor C.H. Park was in favor of extending the trail, but the Forest Service could not do it alone. Its budget and staff were small. Awareness of Mount Baker as a tourist attraction and of all the economic benefits that it could bring was increasing in local communities. The citizens of Deming made contributions for what came to be called the Deming Trail. The Bellingham Chamber of Commerce pitched in for construction of foot logs and bridges. Rangers Joe Ridley and Carl Bell surveyed the trail and supervised the work. The trail was ready when sixty Mazamas (club membership was smaller now that The Mountaineers had split off) arrived early in August.

Several members of the group who lived in Bellingham arranged for a welcome and entertainment in that community. Then a long file of climbers and packhorses headed up the trail assisted by Rangers Ridley and Bell, who showed them a good campsite. An open, parklike area at timberline was selected for base camp—Camp Gorman—and parties set out to explore the area. One group immediately came upon a beautiful region of subalpine meadows which they named, predictably, Mazama Park—"fifty acres of sunshine, red and white heather, rare alpine flowers and hungry butterflies."[11] Another party, led by veteran John A. Lee, wandered high on the mountain exploring the glaciers. Names had not yet been assigned to Baker's southern glaciers, and they wanted to determine how many glaciers there were before they named them. It was difficult to tell from high on the mountain, for the southern slopes seemed encased in one massive sheet of ice. By examining streams running from the base of the glacial mass and configurations of ice at its lower end, however, Lee's group decided there were several glaciers.

When Lee's party came back to camp after their glacial explorations, they held a campfire for the whole group:

> One night, the red glow of the Mazama camp-fire fell upon a group of mountaineers in khaki and corduroy sitting cross-legged before the fire drying their spiked boots—scarlet sweaters and bandannas catching the shifting glow—while three score eager sun-browned faces were upturned to a man in rough mountain garb; a man for whom the arctic snows that crowned Mt. Baker had perpetual fascination, whose zest for exploration had on a former occasion brought him into the very jaws of death there on that crystal dome cutting the heavens.... No man had given himself with such unquenchable zeal to the study and exploration of this peak as Charles F. Easton, who stood among his fellow clubmembers recounting the changes he had noted in this "Great White Watcher" of the Indians.... As he talked, we resolved that for no one else should our newly explored glacier be named.[12]

We can imagine Easton, a wiry Bellingham businessman of fifty-one years, waxing enthusiastic about the mountain that obsessed him. He told the group how, in 1906, he had been sketching the mountain from far to the west, looking at it through a telescope, when massive avalanches came off the western side, completely changing its appearance. The ice and rock slid off at the precise moment of the great San Francisco earthquake; Easton speculated that there may have been some connection between the two incidents. He told them the history of the mountain as he knew it, and all that he knew about glaciers, which was considerable. And, of course, he described in detail his epic traverse of the mountain the previous summer.

Easton was born in Michigan in 1858, raised in Iowa and educated as an engineer at Valparaiso University in Indiana. He enjoyed a varied career as teacher, mining engineer, geologist, bridge-builder, assayer, inventor and jeweler. He had been granted the first x-ray tube patent in the United States. He taught himself jewelry artisanship and moved west to Wallace, Idaho, where he opened a jewelry store and rose to prominence in the community, eventually becoming a state senator.

Wallace was not a very stable town in the nineteenth century, and his tenure there ended when striking miners blew up a mill and paralyzed the town with violence. Easton moved to Seattle and then, in 1900, to Bellingham, where he opened another jewelry store. Soon he embarked on his studies of Mount Baker. He joined the Mazamas and was on Mount Baker every year. He became the recognized expert on the mountain. When, in 1911, a group of local leaders formed the Mount Baker Club to promote development of the Mount Baker region, Easton was named historian of the group. For the next twenty years, until his death in 1931, Easton studied and wrote about the mountain extensively. He surveyed it, preparing a map that later amazed United States Geological Survey topographers with its accuracy and detail. He collected material about the mountain in a huge scrapbook, which became Exhibit A in the push to make the Mount Baker region a national park. He was chief lobbyist in Washington, D.C. for this proposal, which was ultimately side-tracked by international events. So it was perhaps more appropriate than they realized at the time for the Mazamas to name their new glacier for Charles Finley Easton.

The 1909 Mazama outing's most significant contributions to Mount Baker's history occurred more around the campfires than on the slopes of the mountain. In addition to naming Easton Glacier, they also named Deming Glacier, in tribute to the town that had assisted with the trail construction that made the outing possible. They named a buttress of the Black Buttes for their leader John A. Lee—Lee Promontory; creeks were named for the helpful rangers Joe Ridley and Carl Bell. At one campfire a resolution was offered that Mount Baker, Mount Shuksan and the Sisters Range be "forever preserved as a national park."[13] The idea had first been tossed about at the campfires of the 1906 outing, but the club at that time was more deeply involved with trying to make Crater Lake, in Oregon, a national park. The resolution in 1909 was the real beginning of an effort to preserve Mount Baker and surrounding peaks.

Between campfires the Mazamas did climb the mountain. Several parties went up the Easton and Deming glaciers; some enthusiasts climbed the mountain two and even three times. The "official" ascent departed for the summit on August 11. Thirty-eight climbers ultimately reached the top.

The ropes were not uncoiled. President Gorman had announced that they would make this ascent without the life-line. No mishaps occurred, but

A large summit party, typical of the era

the incident is indicative of the light regard people had at the time for the threat of hidden crevasses, an attitude that would cause problems in years to come.

The Mazama climb was a great success. Before they headed back down the Deming Trail, fifty-four of the sixty people in camp reached the summit. No difficult climbing was done, no new routes pushed up, but the 1906 "failure" was erased when so many Mazamas walked upon the mountain's summit snows. A new region of the mountain had been extensively explored, and the new trail opened a marvelous alpine playground for generations to come.

Before the Mazamas came in 1906, all parties had been small. They had quite a struggle to make their climbs. There were no trails, and the approaches to the mountain were often as difficult as the climb itself. The three club climbs opened up Mount Baker both physically and psychologically. Trails were built, and over a hundred people climbed onto the summit plateau. The 1908 and 1909 climbs were so uneventful that people began to think of Mount Baker, at least over the commonly climbed routes, as an easy climb. This view would soon have interesting consequences.

Two other ascents during the years dominated by the clubs should be mentioned. Many climbs were made each year after 1909; most of them accomplished nothing new of significance. But two climbs are important because they, too, indicate the new attitudes about the mountain. In 1907 Joe Morovits once again led a group to the summit up the Boulder Glacier. Six young men from Bellingham helped Joe with his haying so that he would be free to make the climb. Once they were under way the group climbed with speed, making the ascent from timberline in five and a half hours. They had so much time to kill on the summit that they waltzed over and climbed Sherman Peak, claiming the first ascent (though it probably was not). They returned to the summit of Baker, which required more climbing, then descended to snowline in one hour and twelve minutes. Descriptions of their trip emphasize its speed.

In 1908 another local party left Bellingham on July 21. They were back in town, having reached the summit, in three days, 15 hours and 15 minutes. The fact that they recorded their time so exactly indicates that parties were now vying with each other for speed records. This racing mentality shows that people were thinking of Mount Baker in very different terms than had their predecessors. This new view would reach its apex in a few years—with the Mount Baker Marathons.

7

The Marathons

Mount Baker is getting a formal introduction to the people of our Republic. This mountain and its immediate environs are deserving of improvement and development for its scenic value. It is the object of the Mount Baker Club to continue these marathons as long as they may be beneficial in stirring up active interest and co-operation in the building of roads and better trails which will aid in opening up the fascinating features of the WONDERLAND.

—Charles Finley Easton, 1911

Perhaps the most remarkable chapter in the story of Mount Baker concerns the Marathons.[1] The idea of a race to the summit was the brainchild of the Mount Baker Club, a group of businessmen in Bellingham who joined together to promote tourism and development in the Mount Baker region. Inspired by the example of Mount Rainier, which had become a national park in 1899 and was rapidly becoming a tourist attraction of great benefit to business in communities near it, the Mount Baker Club set out to draw the nation's attention to its mountain. An editorial in the local newspaper summarized the motivation and aspiration of the group.

> There is no better advertising feature than the mountain and island scenery hereabouts. If these things were brought to the attention of the pleasure-seeking Americans from the eastern and middle states there would be a mighty stream of travel this way. And these men and women are usually looking for investments and changes of location while traveling about the country on pleasure bent....[2]

114

Poster promoting the 1912 Mount Baker Marathon

In 1911 the Mount Baker Club thought of a gimmick that would start the flow of people and money—a Mount Baker Marathon.

Appropriately enough, the race would begin at the Chamber of Commerce in downtown Bellingham. Racers would have their choice of conveyance to their choice of trail up the mountain. They could take a special train up the Bellingham Bay and British Columbia Railroad forty-four miles to Glacier on the North Fork of the Nooksack River and run to the mountain's summit over the fourteen-mile Glacier Trail route. Or they could drive by car the twenty-six miles to Heisler's Ranch on the Middle Fork, then run the 16 miles up the Middle Fork to the summit. The latter course was longer but of gentler grade. The race would pit not only the men but the machines they used against one another. The two trails would be competing as well: the people of Glacier would build the trail up Glacier Creek, and they wanted to prove that their trail was the best way up the mountain. An influx of mountain climbers and hikers would, after all, be very good for their new but growing community. So the race was not just good advertising and an

Joe Galbraith near the end of the run at Heisler's Ranch

athletic competition, it was a test of technologies and community spirit and organization as well.

Fourteen stalwarts lined up for the start of the first race at 10 p.m. on Thursday, August 10, 1911. The late evening start would allow the runners to climb the mountain at night when the snow was hard, which presumably would be easier and safer than during the day. The weather was ideal. Parties from Deming and Glacier had been out working on the trails and reported them to be in prime condition. Judges were poised at timberline, ready to climb to the summit to check the racers who got that far. Each racer carried a certificate to be countersigned by judges at the summit and at the finish line back in Bellingham. Fifteen "guards" were stationed at intervals along the trails to discourage cheating. Thousands of spectators lined the streets for the start.

The starting gun barked and six racers roared off in automobiles, probably the first stripped-down hotrods ever to travel Bellingham streets. The drivers took the first corner on two wheels and roared down a straightaway

Marathon Routes 1911~1913

Glacier Route — Train — Foot
Deming Route — Auto — Foot

SUMAS
GLACIER
Mt. Baker
Heisler's Ranch
Mazama Park
BELLINGHAM
Nooksack River
North Fork Nooksack River
Middle Fork Nooksack River
South Fork Nooksack River
Present Day Mt. Baker Highway

and across the railroad tracks, barely beating the train carrying the other eight racers. The crowd cheered them on then went home to bed or settled down to other diversions to pass the time until the finish. No one knew how long the wait would be—the record for the round-trip from Bellingham to the summit and back was 33 hours.

The train reached Glacier in fifty-three minutes and the eight racers hit the trail. They faced a round-trip of approximately twenty-eight miles, half of it uphill with an elevation gain of some 9700 feet (an average of 347 feet to the mile, though the grade was not even all the way). Among the Glacier racers was Harvey Haggard, a woodsman and logger from Glacier. Haggard wore light clothing and tennis shoes for the trail run to timberline, where he would change to calked logging boots for the run across the glaciers.

The men in automobiles reached Heisler's ranch well before the train arrived in Glacier. Jumping out, they stripped off the heavy clothing they wore to protect them from the wind chill of their speedy ride in the open cars. They faced a thirty-two mile run, with an elevation gain like that of their opponents, but the grade of their route was considerably less for most of the way.

The competitive field was narrowed considerably by the time the runners reached the glaciers. All but six had succumbed to injury, exhaustion or common sense. The first runner to reach the top was N.B. Randall of Glacier, coming over the Glacier Trail route. Harvey Haggard was close behind. Joe Galbraith was the first to reach the judges by the Deming Trail.

As the race progressed a strong, cold wind began to blow. The judges on the summit endured it as long as they could, then retreated to a protected spot on the rim of the crater. This became a problem for Turner Riddle who came up the Deming Trail. "When I got near the top the judges were blue with cold," said Riddle.

> I knew I was beat, but wanted to reach the summit. The judges took forty minutes off my time and sent me back again. It was not my fault I did not get to the top. My carbide light gave out and for ten miles I stumbled along the trail in the dark. I held a candle which lasted me for four miles, but this did not give much light.[3]

Five racers registered at the summit before the judges were forced down out of the wind.

Harvey Haggard was running well. After checking in on the summit behind Randall, he steadily gained on him and beat him to the train by

Joe Galbraith boards "Betsy" for the dash to Bellingham with his driver, Hugh Diehl.

Harvey Haggard (in robe), grim because his train derailed after hitting a bull

several hundred feet. The rule was that the first man to the train got it for the final leg back to Bellingham. So Haggard roared off down the track leaving poor Randall, who had run a great race, to cool his heels in Glacier.

Haggard's dreams of glory were premature. A few miles down the track the speeding train with its engine, tender and single car hit a large bull that was astride the track, derailed and tipped onto its side. Haggard was more than thirty miles from the coveted finish. No one was hurt. The crew tried to call a speeder, a small gasoline-powered railroad maintenance vehicle, but could not get one quickly enough for the determined Haggard. He caught a buggy on the road nearby, and the driver lashed his horse at a run for thirty minutes. Haggard commandeered a saddle horse when the beleaguered buggy horse gave out. A few miles down the road at Kendall, he was thrown from that horse into the dust. Remarkably uninjured by all of these mishaps, he was then picked up by an automobile, which finally carried him without further serious mishap to the finish.

Meanwhile Joe Galbraith made good time down the Deming Trail. His Ford and its driver, H.W. Diehl, were waiting for him at Heisler's for the race to Bellingham. Diehl's car, "Betsy," reached more than fifty miles per hour on the straight stretches, quite a pace in those days. Galbraith registered at the Chamber of Commerce twelve hours and twenty-eight minutes after the start. Haggard, despite all of his mishaps, came in just thirty-two minutes later to take second place. Turner Riddle finished third. The Deming Trail and the automobile had won. Galbraith collected the first prize, a whopping sum of one hundred dollars and a buffalo robe.

The first race had been a great success. Thousands had witnessed it. The advertising potential was clear. The Mount Baker Club, editors of local newspapers and the Chamber of Commerce were certain that they had struck a bonanza. An editorial in the *American-Reveille*, Bellingham's leading newspaper at the time, expressed this view in July of the next year as the community prepared for the second race.

> The Mount Baker Marathon, with its attendant features, continues to grow in importance as a great Western festival. Started only a year ago it is already well known in almost every city on the

Joe Galbraith: "Now we're in real trouble, Hugh."

Judges erecting their summit shelter, 1912

Pacific Coast and news of the great event is gradually creeping into all parts of the United States . . . . The fact that it is spectacular and entirely without parallel in the world, is a decided advertising advantage. By all means the Marathon should be made an annual event. It is typically Western, something that stirs a red-blooded generation and one of the biggest assets of Bellingham.[4]

An annual event it would be. The 1912 race was scheduled to start at 11 p.m. on July 24.

Several rule changes were made to improve the race. The 1911 race had been open only to entrants from the three Northwest Washington counties. A new rule opened it to runners from anywhere in the world; organizers hoped world-class runners would enter. A second change was made to avoid a collision of cars and train at the crossing near the start. The autos were given a one-minute head start. Racers were encouraged to have attendants at any and all points in the race, as long as these attendants did not transport the racer. "The committee recommends that all contestants be accompanied by at least one other person above the timberline."[5] As impractical as this was, it indicated concern for the safety of the racers among the crevasses on the upper mountain. This time the judges would erect shelters on the summit and stay there the night of the race. Finally, gasoline speeders would be provided for the second, third and fourth men down the Glacier Trail. Four places would win cash prizes; the first prize was five hundred dollars, a very large sum for the times. Race officials hoped the purse would attract some truly outstanding competitors.

One problem with the first marathon as a spectator event was that once the racers had left the start, little was known of them until they neared the finish. To follow their progress, it was decided to string a telephone line from Glacier, where it could be connected to an existing line, to the summit of the mountain along the race course. Phones could be installed every two miles over this fourteen-mile line, and progress up the Glacier Trail could be monitored. The Deming Trail was too long for such a setup, though plans were made to run a line at least to Mazama Park along that trail.

A full program of events was planned for the three-day festival, and the large purse did attract some accomplished athletes: Jimmy Fitzgerald of Calgary, Alberta, winner of many long-distance races and a Canadian Olympian in 1908; Paul Westerlund of San Francisco, a twenty-seven-year-old marathon champion and immigrant from Finland; Victor Norman, a thirty-seven-year-old veteran of many long-distance races. Local entrants included "Johnny" Magnusson, a tough timber cruiser who had raced the previous year, Harvey Haggard and Turner Riddle, determined to better their 1911 showings, and Victor Galbraith, cousin of the great Joe. But Joe himself had broken a shoulder in an auto crash near Heisler's Ranch while training only two weeks before the second race. All of these racers were on the mountain for weeks before the race, training and plotting the best course among the crevasses.

The telephone line was strung to timberline; the remaining wire would be stretched to the top just before the race. Three hundred small American flags were carried up to mark the trails. The judges climbed to the summit and erected their shelters. They carried up a red lantern and an American flag. The lantern would guide the racers who reached the summit before dawn, the flag those who came after daylight. They also carried "red fire powder," which they would light at the appointed starting time in hopes that spectators in Bellingham would be able to see the other end of the course.

As race day approached, a carnival atmosphere enveloped the whole region. Three U.S. Navy cruisers steamed in and anchored in Bellingham Bay. The Sells-Floto Circus spread its tents. Balloon ascensions and parachute jumps competed with war canoe races and other water events for the attention of the crowds, estimated by some as high as sixty thousand (more realistically probably in the fifteen to twenty thousand range). Thousands of yards of green and white bunting, the colors of the Mount Baker Club, decorated the city, and American flags flew everywhere. Judges, guides, spectators and attendants all stationed themselves on the mountain.

The crowds gathered; the machines to carry the runners were given their final inspections and lined up for the start. Then, to the shock of everyone involved, summit judges J. Will Collins and Nathan L. Davis called over the Glacier Trail telephone to say that they had been turned back at timberline by a raging storm. Conditions on the mountain were terrible. Several feet of new snow had fallen and below snowline the trails were torrents. The

Spent marathon runner reaches trailhead

road from Deming to trailhead at Heisler's Ranch was a quagmire impassable to automobiles. Collins and Davis refused "to send men to their deaths."[6] The race would have to be postponed.

Though the centerpiece of the marathon festival was thereby removed, everyone in town enjoyed themselves. The Navy ships hosted thousands of visitors. All manner of land and water races were run, and festival promoters considered it a success. Meanwhile, the storm continued to pound the high country. We can imagine the racers' disappointment; some were on a tight schedule and would now miss the race.

On Saturday the 27th the mountain appeared from the clouds. It was white with new snow, but the weather reports were good. The race would be run on the 31st. Postponement had reduced the number of racers from sixteen to nine, and these stalwarts lined up to go. The judges reported from the saddle below the summit (as far as the telephone line finally reached) that the weather was again poor but much better than it had been. The starting gun was fired at 11 p.m. and off they went. Three roared away in automobiles for the Deming Trail, the rest on the train to Glacier.

The judges camped in their shelters on the summit as originally planned. They erected their lantern and flag on a pole, but the driving mist thwarted all attempts to light the lantern. Visibility was very poor, but the three hundred flags placed along both routes helped the racers greatly. Even with the flags, though, some had problems finding their way.

Without lantern light, the judges shouted constantly to guide the racers to them in the darkness and mist. At about 4:30 their shouts were answered and the bedraggled form of Paul Westerlund staggered out of the mist. Coming up the Glacier Trail, he had lost his way after reaching the saddle a thousand feet below the summit. He eventually relocated the flags but was near collapse when he reached the judges. His wet clothes were freezing to him. He wore light canvas shoes with spikes on the soles, and his arms were bare to the elbows. The judges tried to warm him and gave him a cup of hot coffee before he wandered back into the gloom.

A few minutes after Westerlund departed, Joe Frankoviz arrived in better shape and shouted to the judges that they had better go down and help Harvey Haggard, who had collapsed on the upper part of the Roman Wall. As they started for him, Haggard came into view, his name well fitting his condition. The judges wondered if he could continue the race, but he seemed to recover quickly with the hot coffee and the realization that the rest of the race was downhill. He was soon off in pursuit of Westerlund and Frankoviz. Victor Galbraith, the last of the Glacier Trail runners still in the competition, checked in, too.

Meanwhile Johnny Magnusson and Turner Riddle were battling their way up the Deming Trail. Hugh Galbraith, another cousin and the third racer on this route, dropped out at timberline. Riddle and Magnusson registered on the summit four minutes apart but almost an hour behind those who had come up the other route. The two raced back down the mountain and jogged to their automobiles shoulder to shoulder after thirty-two miles of racing.

Paul Westerlund had a ten-minute lead on his closest rival when he checked off the summit, but on the downward trail he gradually lost ground to Frankoviz, Haggard and Galbraith, who all passed him three miles from Glacier. They did not realize that they were witness to a remarkable display of grit and courage, for Westerlund had fallen on steep ice on the way up and sustained internal injuries and a broken rib. They thought he was just worn out, as they were. When the leaders passed the two-mile mark, a phone call went down to Glacier informing them there that it would probably be a tight finish at the train. The engineer began to build his head of steam, and the conductor and brakeman stretched a rope at the rear of the coach.

Two racers emerged from the forest, splattered from head to toe with mud, running shoulder to shoulder. Frankoviz seemed to surge ahead. Then Haggard, probably remembering his frustrations of the previous year, summoned a final reserve of energy and just beat him to the rope. They had been racing (running, walking, stumbling, sliding or otherwise moving) for seven hours and thirty-eight minutes. A newspaper reporter described the scene at the train as Haggard and Frankoviz climbed aboard.

> "Wait for Vic," both men murmured, as if with one breath. At that moment Victor Galbraith came dashing into sight down the trail. His stride was long and fast, but he surged from one side of the trail to the other. . . . The Concrete athlete's running suit, which had been of snowy white when he left the train, was now fairly reeking with black muck. He, like his rivals, had stumbled and fallen headlong scores of times on the terrific race down the trail.[7]

Race planners had specified that the train was to wait one minute after the first runner reached it. If more than one made it to the train all the better, for they would then have to race the two blocks to the Bellingham Chamber of Commerce Building. The spectators would love it. The racers themselves had other ideas, agreeing that they would place in the order in which they reached the train. They would jog to the finish in that order to delight the people, but the race was over, at least between them.

The train steamed into Bellingham, this time without tangling with any livestock, thanks to volunteers who patrolled the rails. The three runners tumbled out of the car and made for the finish to the applause of thousands. Harvey Haggard checked in with an incredible elapsed time of nine hours and fifty-one minutes. The other two were only seconds behind. They had traveled eighty-eight miles by train and roughly twenty-eight miles on foot. The record was lowered by two hours and thirty-seven minutes. All six finishers, the first four of whom had run over the Glacier Trail (Westerlund fin-

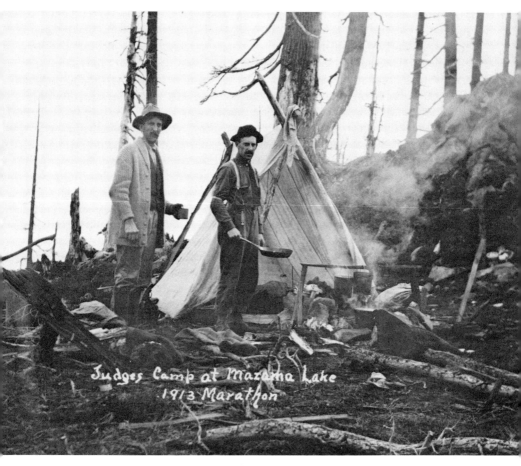

Judges Camp at Mazama Lake
1913 Marathon

While some judges camped on the snow, others enjoyed all the comforts of home

ished despite his injuries), bettered the previous record.

Despite its postponement the second marathon had been a roaring success, at least in the opinion of most people. There were some who began to doubt the wisdom of running around on glaciers at night in poor weather. As a promotional stunt the race was unquestionably a success, but it was becoming clear that the racers were pushing themselves to extremes. Johnny Magnusson lost eleven pounds in his eleven-hour effort. Westerlund had been injured in his fall. Drivers told of runners jogging senselessly past waiting cars at the Deming Trail. Teammates had to catch and carry them to the autos, tying them in their seats so that they would not fall from the open cars.

Still, these unusual men showed remarkable recuperative powers. Turner Riddle rode his bicycle twenty miles before and after his marathons. Joe

Galbraith went home to do his chores after his win the first year. No one suffered any lasting ill effects from participation in the first two races. Promoters still visualized the marathon as an ever-growing annual event.

The third marathon was scheduled for August 15, 1913. Concern for the welfare of the racers grew as people reflected on the risks revealed by the previous race. More changes were made to make it safer. Runners this time would be required to halt for twelve minutes at snowline to put on warm clothing. When they reached car or train they would change again to dry clothes. The start was scheduled for 5 a.m. so that the race could be run entirely in daylight. Finally, runners would go up one trail and descend the other.

This time there were twelve entrants. All would use both car and train, thereby equalizing the mechanical dimension of the race. It had been clearly established in the two previous races that the Glacier Trail, while steeper, was the faster way to go. Since everyone would cover the same ground, the 1913 contest would truly be one of strength and endurance. Nathan L. Davis was again a summit judge, and again he decided at the last minute that the weather was too bad to stage the race. There was much new snow, it was raining, and the judges did not dare venture up the mountain to mark the route. This time Davis was in Mazama Park, on the Deming Trail, and after telling race officials back in Bellingham (a phone line was strung on this trail) that the race should be postponed, he, another judge and a Seattle newspaper reporter went back to the Mount Baker Club cabin in Mazama Park to wait out the storm. They were sure the race would be called off. Before long the weather cleared a bit, and the three set off down the trail.

Before they had gone very far they were aghast to see Paul Westerlund, Joe Frankoviz and Lester Vaughn running up the trail toward them. The race was on after all. The two startled judges stopped the runners, told them of conditions, that the route was not marked and that no judges were on the mountain to check them in. They advised them to go only over the saddle, rather than make the final steep climb to the summit. They then hustled back up the trail and gave the racers what warm clothing they could before they set out up the snow. The runners quickly disappeared up the mountain into the mist.

The racers coming up the Glacier Trail, led by Johnny Magnusson, did not know that the judges had instructed the racers on the other trail to go only through the saddle. They most likely reached the saddle up the shorter route without meeting Westerlund and the others, so proceeded on up to the summit. Magnusson, Victor Norman, Victor Galbraith and A.M. Burnside all found themselves together on the summit with no judges anywhere to be seen. The fog was thick, the wind blowing hard and very cold. The four were concerned because there was no sign of anyone from the Deming side. Burnside agreed to stay a while on the summit to check any others that might come to the top, and the other three started down Deming Glacier.

Magnusson had been over the route many times in practice runs and knew the glacier well; he soon left the other two behind. At snowline Davis and his crew, now comprised of members of the runners' support teams and forest ranger Joe Ridley, were watching anxiously. Magnusson passed, then Victor Norman, who told them to watch for Vic Galbraith, who might be in trouble. After a while Burnside appeared out of the fog. The crew asked him if he had seen Galbraith. He had not, and he confirmed their fears that Galbraith was not where he should be. Burnside suggested that Vic might have passed around the judges somehow and was on the trail. But Davis, nervous about the whole situation, angrily told Burnside that he doubted that was possible, then immediately dispatched a rescue party up the mountain.

As the three runners had come down the mountain, Galbraith had found himself slipping behind. Trying to gain a few feet, he tried a shortcut, only to fall forty feet into a hidden crevasse. Miraculously he broke no bones. He found that he could stand on a snow bridge in the crevasse, and by jogging gingerly and waving and slapping his arms he was able to stay reasonably warm. Five hours after he descended into his dark glacial den he heard the shouts of his cousin Joe and forest ranger Ridley, who quickly dropped a rope to him and hauled him up, cold and bruised but none the worse for wear. It was a close call. The rule change requiring the warm clothing helped him. So had Victor Norman's feeling that something was wrong. Judge Davis' prompt action and the good luck of the search party in finding

Rescue in 1913

129

the small hole through which Galbraith had fallen all prevented what might well have been a fatality.

While all of this was happening on the glacier, Paul Westerlund was running a good race and was first back to Bellingham, in nine hours and thirty-four minutes. He was followed by Frankoviz, then Magnusson. Needless to say, Magnusson was upset at the confusion that had rendered the final placing meaningless. He had gone to the summit—the other two had merely gone over the saddle as they had been instructed. In the end, race officials decided to award first prizes of four hundred dollars to both Magnusson and Westerlund.

The third marathon left bitterness and controversy. Judge Davis was furious. He wrote a lengthy letter to the Bellingham *American-Reveille* explaining his view of what had happened. He would, he said, have nothing to do with any future races, since marathon organizers seemed to be more concerned about the spectators than about the racers. It was simply luck, he pointed out, that had saved Victor Galbraith from death.

Some contended that Paul Westerlund had not won the race fairly, despite the two first prizes. These doubters suggested that if challenged head-to-head by local runners he would lose. A.M. Burnside challenged Westerlund to a race from Glacier to the summit and back. Burnside was a tough trapper who had given up his chance for the prize money when he agreed to wait on the summit for other runners. He was confident that he could win, having led all the way up the Glacier Trail to the summit; Westerlund had come up the other way.

The rematch was run in early September, Burnside leading most of the way, only to be overtaken by Westerlund with just three miles to go. Westerlund's winning time was six hours and two minutes over the twenty-eight-mile course with its 9,700 foot elevation differential. He certainly dispelled any doubts about his strength, though Burnside later claimed to have had such a bad ankle that his doctor had advised him not to race.

This was the last race up Mount Baker. The Mount Baker Club could not promote a race as risky as the marathon had proven to be. In July, just before the third race, a climber from British Columbia had fallen into a crevasse and died. Victor Galbraith's close call reiterated the message of that misadventure. If the race were continued it would only be a matter of time before a marathon-related death would occur.

Marathon promoters were unrealistic in their belief that people could play games on the mountain's upper slopes. In the years before the first race climbers had been making ever-faster climbs to the summit, and no one was having any great difficulty. Even safety-conscious groups like the Mazamas were going up without ropes. There seemed to be no great danger. Speed-climbing of the peak seemed a reasonable thing to do. Still, the promoters knew the dangers. They had hoped that racers would have companions on the glaciers; they made rules to reduce hazards; they cautioned racers about specific hazards. But despite their awareness, their enthusiasm and booster-ism overcame their anxieties. They did everything they could, but storms and hidden crevasses were impossible to control. Mount Baker, they found, was unpredictable even in the summer. Mountaineers of course knew this, but they were a small part of the population, even of the membership of the Mount Baker Club. The Mount Baker Marathon was instructive for many people. Even though the mountain was easily accessible, the climbers well trained and experienced, their equipment the latest and very best, a climb up a mountain as large as Mount Baker is always governed by the vagaries of nature. To deny these vagaries can be an invitation to disaster.

In 1972 the marathon served as the inspiration for another race. Over the years since the first marathons there have been proposals to revive the race, but the problem of safety has always been raised. The race initiated in 1972 was again the brainchild of local boosters, but this time it did not in-volve the high mountain itself. Skiers, runners, cyclists, canoeists and even-tually sailors have raced from "ski" to "sea," covering approximately seventy miles in a relay that descends five thousand feet from the Mount Baker Ski Area. This race, part of a community festival in Bellingham, has been enor-mously successful. It too is subject to the vagaries of weather, but not the ex-tremes of the high mountains. If the Galbraiths, Harvey Haggard and the other Mount Baker Marathon runners could witness today's race, they would think it pretty tame, though by current standards it is a demanding and strenuous event.

8

Parks, Roads and Resorts: 1913-1930

The natural resources must be developed and preserved for the benefit of the many, and not merely for the profit of a few. We are coming to understand in this country that public action for public benefit has a very much wider field to cover and a much larger part to play than was the case when there were resources enough for every one. . . .
— Gifford Pinchot, 1910

The years that followed the marathons were relatively quiet for Mount Baker. Climbers continued to visit the mountain in increasing numbers, but the pioneering had been done. For many years after the races, there were no newsworthy ascents. The Forest Service continued to develop its management policies and to increase its influence in the area. People in Bellingham continued to regard the mountain as a great commercial asset and sought ways to take advantage of it. Their efforts to open and develop the area provide the significant story of the decade following the marathons.

When the Mount Baker Club was formed in 1911 to promote use of the scenic resources of the Mount Baker region, its purposes were clearly stated in its constitution. Foremost was the following:

The objects of this organization shall be to make known and draw public attention to the unrivaled scenic beauties of the MT. BAKER REGION; to establish

Early Forest Service packtrain

camps or resorts which will be available to mountain climbers, tourists and those seeking outdoor enjoyment and recreation; to construct trails and highways and to secure national, state, county and public aid for the construction of such roadways; and, to collect photographic and engineering data, general historic, scientific, botanic, geologic, and other information pertaining to said region.

The club's first big effort to pursue these "objects" was the staging of the marathons, which certainly drew attention. When the decision was made to discontinue the annual marathon, the club sought new ways to pursue their many goals (particularly that of economic development) and found one in the idea of a national park. Mount Rainier National Park was a good example. Established in 1899, it was becoming a national scenic attraction. Resorts were being built near it, and people were traveling there from all over the United States for vacations and adventure. Mount Baker promoters had similar visions for their mountain.

The idea had occurred to some members of the Mazamas' 1906 outing. During their 1909 outing to the mountain the club acted on the idea by drafting a resolution:

> Resolved by the Mazamas, at a meeting called by the president of the Club at Camp Gorman, on Mount Baker, on the evening of August 7, 1909, that a petition be presented to the Hon. Secretary of the Interior respectfully requesting that Mount Baker, Mount Shuksan and their immediate environs . . . be set aside, dedicated and forever preserved inviolate by the Government of the United States as a park for all the people to be called "The Mount Baker National Park."[1]

The resolution went on to suggest that "merchantable timber" on the public lands in the area be harvested and the proceeds used to construct a road and other improvements on the Middle Fork of the Nooksack. The resolution, though not very specific as to what precise area the proposed park should encompass, was duly forwarded to the Secretary of the Interior. A copy was sent to the Secretary of Agriculture, under whose jurisdiction the Forest Service managed the land.

Another resolution to establish a park in the Mount Baker region was introduced in the Washington State Legislature in 1909. The area recommended for inclusion comprised eight townships in the northwestern corner of the Washington National Forest, covering the entire Mount Baker Mining District, Hannegan Pass, and the North Fork of the Nooksack River and all of its tributaries. This resolution, not surprisingly, stirred up strong opposition among miners struggling to establish lucrative operations in the region. Among other things, they feared that a park would interfere with their plans to build roads through some of the most scenic areas to get their minerals to market.

The resolutions must have stirred some interest among the bureaucrats and politicians in Washington, D.C., too. In March of 1910 the district forester wrote to the chief forester that he thought the national park idea was a poor one. It would, he thought, curtail development and timber sales. "The existence of the National Forest sufficiently protects the area, while leaving its resources available for development."[2] Despite the district forester's views, the Forest Service considered the idea for three years, even to the point of proposing specific boundaries. Headed by Gifford Pinchot and then by Henry Graves, the Forest Service was philosophically opposed to parks in general. These foresters were guided by the idea that public lands should be managed for many purposes under a plan of balanced use. Parks involved preservation of scenery, which often precludes other uses. Further, parks were administered by the Department of the Interior, and Pinchot had struggled for years to have the forest reserves transferred to the Department

Detailed 1912 Mount Baker map, as drawn by C.F. Easton

of Agriculture. Since he had accomplished this in 1905, his agency and department had resisted transfer of any land under their jurisdiction back to Interior.

Despite this resistance, the Forest Service apparently thought that Mount Baker would inevitably become a national park, so they sought to minimize the impact on their jurisdiction by proposing rather limited boundaries. Their belief in the probability of park status for the mountain is revealed in the following Forest Service memorandum:

> It is believed that the present conditions surrounding the existing Rainier and Crater Lake National Parks and the territory in the vicinity of Mt. Hood, Mt. Olympus, and Mt. Baker, which are probable locations for future National Parks, require that special attention be given to this matter by the Supervisors of the Forests in the vicinity. Not only should the territory close to the National Parks or probable National Parks be conservatively administered, but lands adjacent to all ways of ingress and egress should also be preserved as nearly as possible in their natural condition.[3]

In June of 1913 the Washington National Forest supervisor presented his park proposal to his superiors. It included approximately fifty thousand acres of "wild, massive, uninhabited, high mountainous country."[4] Most forested areas around the mountain with their merchantable timber were excluded. The Forest Service was ready for the congressional Mount Baker National Park initiative that it felt certain was coming.

Charles Finley Easton, then Historian of the Mount Baker Club, began his initiative in 1915. He had been privately nurturing the idea since 1903, when he began studying and climbing the mountain. He had been in on Mazama discussions; he knew of the Forest Service proposal and considered it too limited. In his opinion, the Forest Service had too few resources and too little interest to be entrusted with the region as a recreational and scenic resource. A national park administered by the Department of the Interior would ensure better development of the area.

The annual banquet of the Twentieth Century Club in Bellingham provided him with a forum. The Honorable Lin H. Hadley, congressman from the district, would be there. Easton, the featured speaker, both presented the national park idea and unveiled his massive Mount Baker Book, a scrapbook in which he had compiled, during his tenure as historian of the Mount Baker Club, historic, scientific, botanic, geologic and other information about the mountain.

"The leaven began to work," as Easton put it later.[5] An outing to the mountain was organized, following Skyline Divide on the new Forest Service trail. Congressman Hadley went along and was honored when the 7,515-foot peak prominent on Chowder Ridge was named for him. (The

Map of first Mount Baker National Park proposal

name "Chowder" also came out of this trip. The group found marine fossils on the ridge that were so complete that Easton made a mock chowder of them for dinner.) Hadley became a proponent of the park idea. The local press was enthusiastic; Easton noted that "It had the approval of everybody, everywhere."[6]

The Mount Baker Club appointed a National Park Committee to work out a detailed proposal. In the fall of 1915 this committee and Congressman Hadley arranged a meeting in Tacoma with Stephen T. Mather, then Special Assistant to the Secretary of the Interior and soon to be Director of the National Park Service, still a year from its creation. Mather, Horace Albright (Mather's young assistant who was one day to succeed him as Director of the Park Service) and other Interior Department officials were touring the nation inspecting parks, promoting the creation of new ones and generally trying to raise public interest in national parks. Others present at the meeting were two veterans of Mount Baker adventure—John A. Lee of the Mazamas and Asahel Curtis of the Mountaineers.

The Federal officials were enthusiastic about the Mount Baker National Park proposal. The only disagreement was whether Mount Shuksan should be included. Mather thought that it should be. The Mount Baker Club committee excluded it "out of consideration for certain mining interests that would be involved."[7] All parties left the meeting dedicated to promoting the best possible park.

When all issues of boundary location were resolved between the committee and the Interior Department, Congressman Hadley prepared and introduced in the House of Representatives "A Bill to Establish the Mount Baker National Park in the State of Washington." On January 22, 1916, an identical bill was introduced in the Senate by Senators Jones and Poindexter. Charles Finley Easton took his huge scrapbook to Washington to lobby for the bill. Hearings were held and reports filed by the Departments of Agriculture and Interior. The former was not happy with the size of the proposed park, for it included merchantable timber. The Department of the Interior was, of course, solidly behind it. The political climate for a park seemed favorable, and supporters were optimistic.

But Mount Baker National Park was not to be. The First World War was grinding on in Europe. The United States was boosting its military preparedness. A debate about American posture toward the European belligerents raged, and a presidential campaign was being waged. Minor matters such as park bills languished in this period of crisis. When, in April of 1917, the United States declared war on the German Empire, all attention was focused on mobilization. The Mount Baker National Park legislation died of neglect.

The impetus for development was much diminished while America was involved in the war. After the war, however, development once again became a priority, especially roads and hotel accommodations. When its

Camp Shuksan, 1930s

Mount Baker Park dream failed to reach fruition, the Mount Baker Club quietly faded from influence. A few dedicated members kept it alive, and it eventually evolved into an outing club, but its days as a major promoter of development were ended.

Charles Finley Easton, however, was still actively pursuing his dreams. In 1921 he addressed the Bellingham Chamber of Commerce and suggested a specific direction for new development.

> Mt. Baker was here when man came; it has been here ever since— yet even today it is accessible only to persons who have the stamina to tread its difficult trails. . . .
>
> The construction of what will ultimately be a fine automobile road into the Mt. Baker region is the first practical step toward enlisting the financial co-operation of visitors in developing the region. When such a road is completed, there will be a definite objective to automobile tourists. . . . It will make a new era in the exploitation of Northwest Washington's scenic attractions, which potentially are worth millions and which cannot be excelled anywhere in the world.[8]

Easton suggested that the best route would be up the North Fork beyond Glacier to Austin Pass. Before the year ended, construction had begun on an eight-foot right-of-way from Excelsior, seven miles beyond Glacier, to Shuksan, where the road would turn uphill if it were to reach Austin Pass. The key to approval of the project was the willingness of the Forest Service to contribute funds for the road (two Federal to each local dollar) if local national park promoters would cease pushing for a park. Since development was the reason why park proponents had supported a park to begin with, they readily agreed. If the Forest Service would do the developing, that was fine with them. So, for a time at least, the Forest Service won its long struggle to retain administration of lands in the Mount Baker region.

Road building progressed and a plan emerged to construct a major hotel near Austin Pass. Local supporters included C.H. Park, supervisor of the National Forest; J.P. McMillan, a county commissioner; Bert Huntoon, the engineer who had first visited Austin Pass in 1893; and Frank Sefrit, managing editor of the Bellingham newspaper. They attracted financiers and formed a corporation, which they called the Mount Baker Development Company. By early 1923 they had signed a lease for a hotel site in Austin Pass Meadows. That summer, using tents, they began their first tourist concession. On a guarantee, backed by a considerable sum of money, that a resort to accommodate tourists would be built on the leased site, the Federal Government agreed to provide funds for construction of a nine-mile road up the hill from Shuksan to the hotel.

Site work in Austin Pass Meadows began in 1924. A dining hall and bunk house, known as the Heather Inn, were built, along with a stone caretaker's cabin. At Shuksan an inn to accommodate fifty people and several cabins were built. Modern, automobile-based tourism had finally come to Mount Baker country. Plans for the hotel were presented in 1925, and construction began. The road to the Meadows, renamed Heather Meadows to eliminate confusion with Austin Pass, far above the construction site, was completed in 1926. The name of the National Forest itself was changed from Washington National Forest to Mount Baker National Forest. The former name was misleading (people "back east" often thought it included more of the state than it did), and hotel promoters argued that the new name would be very helpful in their advertising and publicity efforts. The Forest Service and the development company built trails to serve the hotel clientele. The foresters built a trail around Table Mountain in 1925.

Opening on July 14, 1927, the hotel, called the Mount Baker Lodge, was large and lavish. It was an L-shaped building two hundred and ten feet long and from fifty to one hundred and thirty feet wide with one hundred rooms and a huge dining hall that could seat three hundred. An observation tower rose seventy feet at one end; as many as fifty people could stand at the top and gaze around at the scenery. With the Heather Inn and thirteen cabins, the resort complex could accommodate three hundred guests and the staff to

Mount Baker Lodge

serve them. The development had its own hydroelectric power system and a fleet of buses to carry guests to and from Bellingham. Many dreams were realized on that July evening when three hundred guests enjoyed ceremony, banquet and dancing.

There is no record that Charles Finley Easton, by then getting along in years, played any significant role in the building of the hotel complex. Still, he must have been satisfied that others had taken his vision seriously. The heavily promoted Mount Baker Lodge was busy throughout the summer of 1927.[9] The Forest Service estimated that 11,700 guests visited the lodge that year for the scenery and social life. Saddle ponies carried some guests around Table Mountain. Hikers walked the various trails. Guides were available for climbs of Mounts Shuksan and Baker. Evening entertainment included dancing, movies and songfests. The lodge became a fashionable place for the affluent to visit and vacation.

The Mount Baker Highway and Lodge allowed thousands of people previously denied a visit to the high country an opportunity to gaze at the glacier-hung bastions of Mount Shuksan, to wander in alpine meadows, to

Miniature golf at Mount Baker Lodge

walk the midsummer snows of the high Cascades. But all of this "industrial tourism," as it has come to be called, changed the place. No longer was it the quiet alpine scene it had been when only mountaineers visited Austin Pass. A member of the Mazama outing to the area in 1929 recorded the change.

How strange it must have seemed to the Mount Baker veterans! A splendid inn stands there in the meadows where they had camped in such solitude ten years before. Roads wind through the shallow glacial valley with cabins popping out on every bend. A mile beyond the inn, in the very eye of the pass, cars were parked that day by the scores; the air reeked with their fumes. On yonder sidehill a searing slash marked the creeping advance of human occupation of this wilderness as a noisy power shovel clattered about its business of taking the road across the pass to the shoulder of Table Mountain. Powdermen with their drills rumbled away on the rocks that ten years ago had housed the marmots. Not so long before the mountain goat had trod that bluff. Air compressors droned their song of demolition.[10]

Visitors at Mount Baker Lodge

Mountaineers may have mourned their loss, but for everyone else the changes were good ones. In the 1920s the lodge and road were the only modern intrusion into thousands of acres of high wilderness country.

While all the maneuvering for a park and development of roads and lodges was going forward, mountaineering parties continued to visit Mount Baker itself. The Mountaineers were back in force in 1916. They came fifty strong on the train from Bellingham to Glacier, then proceeded on foot the fourteen miles to the abandoned town of Shuksan, near the mouth of Swamp Creek, on the North Fork of the Nooksack. A six-mile walk up the creek brought them to Twin Lakes, where two thousand gold seekers had pitched their tents. In 1916 the lakes were entirely abandoned. They climbed Winchester Mountain to survey the countryside then visited nearby Lone Jack Mine, which was still being worked. From the lakes they set out for Hannegan Pass at the head of Ruth Creek.

The group did more climbing on their way to the pass than they had intended, for they traversed over the shoulder of Goat Mountain and were forced into some precarious down-climbing to reach the creek. They even-

Mount Baker Highway in its early days

tually reached their destination, where they found "climbing and fishing and visiting for three happy care-free days."[11] They climbed Ruth Mountain, and the ambitious members of the group toyed with the idea of dropping down to the Nooksack River and making an attempt on Mount Shuksan's imposing northern wall. Instead they returned down Ruth Creek to Shuksan and hiked up to Austin Pass. This would be their base camp for the "big climbs" of Mounts Baker and Shuksan.

Both climbs were successful. Montelius Price, who had climbed with Asahel Curtis, led the three-day Mount Shuksan climb over the route the two had pioneered ten years earlier; twenty-five made the ascent. Meanwhile, Curtis led a reconnaissance of Mount Baker. When the Mount Shuksan party returned, thirty aspirants set out for Baker, led by Curtis. They went out Ptarmigan Ridge past Coleman Pinnacle, then onto the glaciers for a long traverse to the cleaver between Boulder and Park Glaciers. The long line of people went up the cleaver, then threaded their way upward between many large crevasses until they reached the summit. The view was good, the descent uneventful; three weeks after they had started, fifty tired but satis-

Mount Baker Lodge, ringed by peaks

fied Mountaineers emerged from the forest at Concrete on the Skagit River. From their Austin Pass camp they had come down Shuksan Creek and Baker River.

At Baker Lake the Mountaineers passed the salmon hatchery built in 1907. All supplies to build and then operate the hatchery had been packed in by mule train from Concrete. The complex consisted of a main hatchery building, barn, tool warehouse, mess hall, twelve-room bunkhouse and foreman's residence. The main building was new, the original having burned to the ground in 1914. The complex was a small scar on the wilderness but a harbinger of developments to come to the Baker River side of the mountain.

Other parties, large and small, climbed Mount Baker during this period. The Normal School in Bellingham (later Western Washington University) started its tradition of summer outings to the mountain. The Mazamas were back in 1920, intending to climb the northeastern side, the route that had eluded so many on the first Mazama outing to the mountain in 1906. In 1920 the road ended at Excelsior, so the group of sixty made a fourteen-mile hike from there to Austin Pass, traveling up from Shuksan over the trail recently built by the Forest Service.

Once again John Lee was a climbing leader. While a scouting party examined Mount Shuksan, he led a similar reconnaissance to the top of Mount Baker. Lee's group found the traveling possible but the route finding complex and did not reach the summit until late afternoon. They spent an unplanned night in a crevasse above Boulder-Park Glacier, as Lee had on the first Mazama outing to the area, but suffered no ill effect. Both scouting groups returned to camp. Mount Shuksan was attempted first, and twenty made the summit. Then forty-one Mazamas and five miners who had joined them tackled Mount Baker; they, too, all reached the top. The outing was a resounding success. Not a drop of rain fell on them during the two-week trip, and all of their goals were achieved except repeating the climb that Curtis, Kiser and their companions had made on the upper Park Glacier in 1906. As climbing leader, Lee opted for a route that many members of the party could manage, for crevasses and steepness made the upper Park Glacier a doubtful path to the summit. Once again the Mazamas thoroughly enjoyed their idyllic campsite in Heather Meadows, innocent of the changes to come.[12]

Changes were taking place, though. Joe Morovits left his Baker Lake haunts in 1918. Perhaps he tired of his solitary life. He had said he would "stay until I could clean up a few hundred thousand dollars."[13] Perhaps he finally admitted to himself that the chances for that were slight. Whatever his reasons, after twenty-seven years of exploration and labor in the country east of the mountain, he disappeared, but not unexpectedly. He had sold his mining claims on Sulphide Creek in 1916 to the Mount Shuksan Molybdenite Mine and Milling Company, which was operated by a group from Seattle. In 1917 he sold his homestead and Fourth of July Mines to a group called the Mount Baker Land and Mine Company, one member of which already held a lien on Joe's stamp mill. The company never worked the mines but used the ranch as a hunting and logging camp.

Joe drifted back to coal mining, where he reportedly earned a princely wage of twenty-five dollars a day as a powder monkey. An accident ended this brief lucrative phase. He was struck and crippled in the mines by a chunk of coal. The joyful mountain man was forced to wear a neck brace, and his health declined. No one knew for sure, but his friends in Concrete— Baker City when Joe first knew the village—believed that he died alone in some city hospital or nursing home, a sad end for the "hermit of Baker Lake" and the mountain's first climbing guide. Yet "he lives, in a way, on his Mount Baker in a hundred stories of derring-do, a kind of Paul Bunyan of the Cascades—Morovits the mighty man."[14]

Others came along to replace him, at least as guides. Visitors to Mount Baker Lodge could hire someone to lead them up either Mount Baker or Mount Shuksan. Head guide was Bill Cochran, a former coal miner turned YMCA Physical Director, an enthusiastic and capable climber. Bill would climb Baker, his favorite mountain, at the slightest provocation. He claimed thirty-nine complete ascents of the peak between 1912 and 1932. In 1960 Cochran, nearly eighty, heard that several men claimed to have made the first complete ascent of Cockscomb Ridge and disputed the claim. He and two companions had climbed it in 1929. He also claimed the first winter ascent of Mount Baker on January 4, 1929.[15]

Among Cochran's fellow guides at the lodge was Ben Thompson, a husky, flamboyant, "Clark Gable type" who specialized in Mount Shuksan climbs. Before he left the area in search of greater fame and fortune as a writer, cartoonist, skier and entrepreneur, he made his mark climbing some new routes on Mount Shuksan. Thompson also was among the first to ski in the Heather Meadows area. It was a long trip up the unplowed road from Glacier, but that didn't stop Thompson. Extensive winter use of the area was many years in the future, but its skiing potential was first revealed to Thompson and his friends.

The guide who enjoyed the longest career in hobnailed boots and skis was Clarence "Happy" Fisher, a small wiry mountain enthusiast who taught school when he was not climbing. (His teaching career nearly ended when he refused for many years to attend summer school because he was too busy climbing.) He left his name on the region. "Hap" and his buddies thought that there must be a shorter route up Mount Shuksan than the long and laborious Curtis Falls route pioneered by Asahel Curtis and Montelius Price on their first ascent. Fisher and Dr. E.P. Spearin, a Bellingham dentist, discovered the gully system on the south flank of the mountain known today as the Fisher Chimneys. They climbed Mount Shuksan by that route in 1927. Fisher was first on the summit of several peaks in the area, among them Colfax, the 9,443-foot satellite summit of Mount Baker. He climbed for decades,

Ben Thompson

Shelter cabin at Mazama Park

became the dean of local mountaineers, and was called upon whenever leadership or rescue was required.

These men and a few others led climbs for pay and for fun, in the irrepressible tradition of Joe Morovits. They were local men who loved the local mountains, grabbing any opportunity to go to the high country. No record exists of the extent of their mountain guide business. Few visitors to the lodge aspired to closer views of the big mountains than those provided from Austin Pass or Artist Point (called Huntoon Point later after the manager of the lodge) just above Heather Meadows. But if they wanted to climb, Fisher and his colleagues were ready to show them the way.

The hotel complex was not the only construction close to the mountain during this era. The Mount Baker Club did some building of its own. Before the 1912 marathon they had constructed a "shelter cabin" at Mazama Park on Ridley Creek, at the head of the Middle Fork of the Nooksack River. This cabin served racers and officials on the Middle Fork race course. The club also hoped to build another cabin somewhere along the Glacier Trail route. In 1912 Henry Engberg and Charles Finley Easton scouted for a site and fixed on Heliotrope Ridge, elevation approximately five thousand feet. Their vision at the time was of a stone structure with six sleeping rooms, a large living room, a double fireplace and a porch all around. It would be close to the glacier.

The club began raising money for the project, but the financial burden of staging the marathon was more than the club had anticipated. It managed to construct a modest shelter on the site Engberg and Easton had selected, but could do no more. After the races were cancelled, the club took a few years to retire race-related debts. When the war interfered with its national park plans, the club almost died. But a few people remained active, including of course Charles Finley Easton, and in the early 1920s the club began to revive. Fund-raising for a cabin was renewed, and support for the project grew. Finally in October of 1925, Kulshan Cabin was dedicated on a tributary of Grouse Creek, ten miles up the trail from Glacier, just below timberline a short distance west of Heliotrope Ridge. It was a log structure that could lodge a substantial party and provide the club and others with a base for climbing and hiking on the mountain.

The effort of constructing the cabin seems to have once again sapped the strength and finances of the members, who were forced to reorganize again in June of 1928, this time incorporating the club. With the old roster of eighty members forming its nucleus, the new corporation assumed the debts of the old club. This new Mount Baker Club, while retaining the long-standing goals of drawing public attention to the scenic beauties of the region and encouraging development and study, declared itself an outing club. In particular, it would promote and engage in mountaineering in the North Cascade Mountains. Among its leaders were Will Pratt of the original 1911 group and young climbers and skiers like Hap Fisher and Dr. Spearin. They

The first Kulshan Cabin, 1925

got things moving, and in 1929 the club scheduled nineteen outings, published a newsletter and carried on the tradition begun nearly twenty years earlier of helping people to enjoy the scenic beauties of the Mount Baker area.

The building of the Mount Baker Highway and the lodge at Heather Meadows was certainly a dream come true for many, particularly for engineer Bert Huntoon and visionary Charles Finley Easton. The resort development, with its roads, guides and skiers, changed the region more abruptly and finally than any event to that date. Climbers continued to flock to Mount Baker, but the pioneering shifted to the rocks and glaciers of Mount Shuksan and other North Cascade peaks.

Joe Morovits' departure marked the end of an era. There had never been much opportunity in the region for independent, solitary, hardy souls like Joe, but a few had tried, with modest means and remarkable perseverance. Joe had failed, as they all had, so he moved on, with little more for his labors than memories of great virgin forests and high mountain scenery. And he was the last; there are no more mysterious and romantic characters like him in the Mount Baker story.

9

Hard Times and Skiers: 1930-1950

*Be it enacted... that for the purpose of relieving the acute
condition of widespread distress and unemployment now
existing in the United States, and in order to provide for the
restoration of the country's depleted resources... the
President is authorized... to provide for employing citizens of
the United States who are unemployed, in the construction,
maintenance and carrying on of works of a public nature
in connection with the forestation of lands belonging to the
United States....*

—The Emergency Conservation Work Act,
March 31, 1933

Early in the morning of August 5, 1931, Bert Huntoon was out in the meadows near Mount Baker Lodge taking pictures of the sunrise. The morning was beautiful. There was little wind. The first rays of the sun would soon strike the high summits to the north. All was still except for a distant roar of water and the pipings of juncoes and chickadees. Suddenly Huntoon's reverie was destroyed by the fire alarm at the lodge. Rushing across the heather, he was shocked to see flames already racing across the roof. Men were shouting and running and struggling with hose lines. Even as he ran for the building it seemed hopeless—the fire had a fast start.

Huntoon and other hotel staff rushed through the burning building yelling and kicking at doors to make sure all guests made

Ruins of Mount Baker Lodge, 1931

their way to safety. The walls of the lobby, dining room and corridors were covered with cedar shakes, which burned furiously. A tank containing nineteen hundred gallons of fuel oil exploded. Soon the building was an inferno as flames leaped hundreds of feet into the air, their roar—almost a shriek—likened by spectators to the sound of a steam whistle. The fire crew with its seven hoses could but stand by and watch, and in two hours the magnificent lodge was a smoking ruin.

The Mount Baker Lodge had lasted only five years, but its impact had been great. Thousands of people had discovered the delights of Heather Meadows, Mount Shuksan and Mount Baker. A good road had been built—ironically, at the time of the fire the highway department was nearing completion of the highway extension three miles beyond Heather Meadows to Artist Point. The thirty-two-room annex, all the guest cabins and the

Heather Inn survived the blaze and could still accommodate one hundred guests. Guests continued to come, but the dazzle and glory of the beautiful hotel was gone. The Development Company, which was really just getting started, could ill afford such a loss, particularly since its insurance only partially covered its quarter-million dollar investment in the resort. On top of this, the nation was in the throes of a deep depression. Few people had the means to visit such a place. The wealthy would have come to the lodge despite the depression, but without the hotel the resort could not offer the glamour and luxury sought by such people. The company never recovered from the fire.

The Development Company may have fallen on hard times, but the recently reorganized Mount Baker Club was going strong. Its members were traveling all over Mount Baker country, led by Hap Fisher and other veterans of its meadows and crags. Parties were vying for the first ski ascent of Mount Baker and several attempts were made during the winter of 1930-31. Skiing was becoming increasingly popular with club members. The Mount Baker Ski Club acquired a cabin, known as Verona Cabin, four miles up the highway from Shuksan on a mining claim. Beginning in 1931, regular winter outings were made for skiing in the Heather Meadows area. Ten such trips were made that winter.

These winter trips were quite an undertaking. Skiers could drive to Glacier and as far beyond as road conditions would allow. In the early 1930s

Skiing near Mount Baker Lodge, late 1920s

the Highway Department made no effort to keep the road open beyond Excelsior, seven miles east of Glacier. When the snow line was low, visitors had to hike or ski another 6.7 miles from there to Shuksan, or 11.7 miles to Verona Cabin. Skiers had to climb with their long wooden skis yet another four miles beyond the cabin to Heather Meadows. Then, if they wanted any downhill runs, they had to "bust the powder" or pack the snow by sidestepping. Mount Baker skiing at this time was a sport only for the strong and dedicated. (From the start, skiing in Heather Meadows was referred to as "skiing Mount Baker." This is a misnomer, for the mountain is several miles away to the south. The meadows are much closer to Mount Shuksan.)

The approach to Heather Meadows continued to be strenuous for skiers through the winter of 1933. In January of that year the Development Company's caretaker at its Shuksan Inn cleared a quarter-mile ski runway there, nine miles below Heather Meadows on the highway. Forty to fifty skiers came up to enjoy it. Snow at Shuksan was three and a half feet deep; the Highway Department was prevailed upon to keep the road open as far as the inn. But heavy snow later in the month defeated the plow crew's somewhat half-hearted efforts (their equipment was sadly inadequate), and once again it was quite a trek to get to good skiing. In September of 1933 the Mount Baker Club made a concerted effort to have the road plowed at least to Shuksan throughout the winter. They had no success, but the numbers going to the meadows for skiing continued to increase regardless of the difficulties of the trip.

The property on which the Verona Cabin stood was sold to a mining company in December of 1934, and while the new owners assured the Mount Baker Club skiers that they could continue to use their cabin, the group decided that such an arrangement was too uncertain to suit them. They formally organized the Mount Baker Ski Club (still affiliated with the Mount Baker Club) and set out to build their own cabin. They designed a forty-by-twenty-foot structure that would sleep up to sixty-five skiers. By December of 1935 it was completed at Camp Four, just below Heather Meadows, on Galena Creek.

By this time the road was finally being kept open to the meadows in winter. In 1934 a Hollywood film company decided that the area was ideal for the filming of "The Call of the Wild," Jack London's story of the far north, starring Clark Gable and Loretta Young. A Klondike village appeared in Heather Meadows in January of 1935, and more than a hundred people worked there on the film.[1] Highway crews, using a new rotary plow, struggled with a series of blizzards to keep the road open, failing at times. When the last of the cameramen left in mid-February, the Highway Department decided to plow the road to the lodge for the rest of the winter. Skiers rejoiced, the lodge remained open all winter and the first full season of winter sports was enjoyed at Heather Meadows. The highway was cleared throughout the winter for the remainder of the decade, until World War II

The Galena Cabin of the Mount Baker Ski Club, near Heather Meadows

made gasoline too scarce to run the plows.

Skiing continued to grow in popularity, drawing increasing numbers of people to Heather Meadows. In May 1935, the Pacific Northwest Ski Association held its first slalom meet at Panorama Dome above Heather Meadows. There were one hundred and thirty skiers in the race, with several thousand spectators. So many skiers ventured to the area that an enterprising logger named Arthur Brandlund designed an "escalator" to transport them up Panorama Dome. This was a hoisting sled that could carry up to twenty persons from an elevation of 4,200 feet to 5,100 feet in less than five minutes. The sled was pulled up the steep slope on a steel cable by a double-drum donkey engine concealed in the trees at the top of the slope. The Forest Service allowed the operator to charge a small fee, which was not to exceed twenty-five cents a trip. Skiers were willing to pay this exorbitant price (it was high for those times); the climb up the face was long, steep and exhausting in unpacked snow. This ingenious contraption had been operating only a month when, early in January of 1936, an avalanche hit Brandlund and

Spring skiing near Mount Baker Lodge, late 1920s

two companions as they made their way up the haul-back cable to start the day's operation. Brandlund was killed and the experiment ended. With the demise of the "escalator," the Development Company decided to try a more conventional ski lift and installed a rope tow.

Five hundred skiers schussed the slopes around the lodge throughout the winter of 1936, and in May as many as a thousand visited the area on a good weekend in hundreds of cars. Promoters waxed eloquent about the potential of this new sport, but they knew that the resort would have to be improved. A bigger and better hotel was essential. The nation was slowly pulling itself out of the Depression, and in 1937 the directors of the Mount Baker Development Company began working with the Forest Service on plans for a new $1.5 million hotel on the site of the ill-fated lodge. The hope was that the Federal Government, through its Works Progress Administration, would build the facility. Despite much hoping and talking, nothing came of the idea.

There were, of course, activities and developments in the Mount Baker region in the 1930s that were unrelated to skiing. The Civilian Conservation Corps (CCC) worked on many projects. This program was established in 1933 by the Roosevelt administration to put young men to work, help them learn useful skills and accomplish needed conservation work throughout the United States. The men, organized into camps administered by the United States Army, worked on public lands with the cooperation and supervision of federal resource-management agencies. There were two camps in the vicinity of Mount Baker, one in the Glacier Ranger District and one in the Baker River District; both worked on Forest Service projects.

The Glacier District camp was established in 1933, first on the banks of the Nooksack River near the tiny village of Shuksan, then on Boulder Creek five miles west of Glacier.[2] Camp Glacier, as it was called, consisted initiąlly of five Army officers and enlisted men and two hundred CCC men, of whom forty-five were "Local Experienced Men" (LEMs). Many LEMs were skilled woodsmen and supervised and instructed groups of "enrollees," younger men who, though physically able, were neither employed nor experienced. The enrollees might come from anywhere in the United States; many in Camp Glacier came from the Midwest.

CCC recruits would start as laborers, then graduate to one of the more specialized crews. Activities were divided into several major areas: timber improvement, soil conservation, construction and fire prevention and suppression. Jobs included carpentry, vehicle maintenance, saw filing, tree trimming and thinning, and trail construction.

CCC crew constructing forest-camp table and benches at Baker Lake, 1936

The Camp Glacier men compiled an impressive list of achievements in their seven years in the District, before the Second World War brought the demise of the program. They built a temporary camp near Shuksan, then a more permanent one at Boulder Creek, several miles west of Glacier. They improved and extended the road toward Hannegan Pass and built a road from Shuksan to within two miles of Twin Lakes. They constructed more than forty-three miles of surfaced truck roads, including those starting up Wells and Canyon Creeks. They developed four lookouts and eleven camp-grounds and expanded the Glacier Ranger Station. A major revegetation effort was launched at Heather Meadows to repair damage caused by too many "social trails" during the heyday of the lodge. And they built a fine structure, the Austin Pass Warming Hut, above the meadows. Trails were constructed and improved, trees pruned, snags felled, telephone lines installed and repaired. More than one hundred miles of telephone lines eventually connected the Glacier Ranger Station and its fire lookouts. Storms constantly damaged these lines, keeping CCC crews busy.

There also was a CCC camp at Baker Lake, though a small one of thirty men. A road had been pushed up Baker River to Baker Lake in the late 1920s and early 1930s. Permanent district headquarters had been established at Koma Kulshan, below Baker Lake. The U.S. Bureau of Fisheries was still

Forest fire training at the Glacier CCC camp, 1933

trying to operate its hatchery at the lake, but heavy snow again flattened the main building. The CCC men built a new hatchery and water system, and operation resumed in 1939. CCC crews also worked to complete recreational development around Baker Lake.

The CCC left a lasting impression on the Mount Baker region. Their road building opened areas previously accessible only to hikers. Eventually some of the roads they started would become major log-hauling thoroughfares. Their construction of lookouts and telephone lines enabled the Forest Service to extend its protective eye and more effectively suppress forest fires. Its campground and trail construction effort provided facilities for the rising public interest in outdoor recreation. Thanks to the CCC, the 1930s may well have been the high-water mark of recreational development in the Mount Baker region.

The 1930s was also the beginning of the era of fire lookouts in the Mount Baker region, which lasted until the last fire guard shuttered the lookout cabin atop Winchester Mountain in 1967. The first fire lookout cabin in the area was built on Church Mountain in 1928. Others were built on Baker Point and Park Butte south of Mt. Baker, and on Excelsior Peak, Winchester Mountain and Goat Mountain to the north. All were built in the 1930s. Fire guards were on duty in some of these places even before cabins

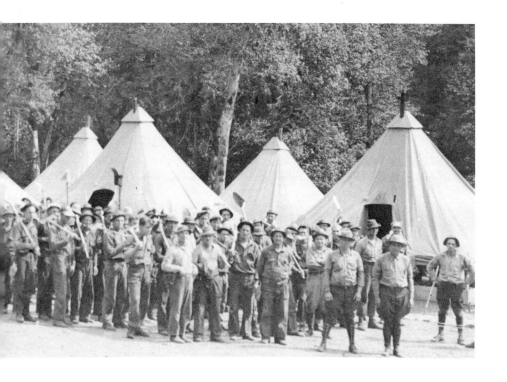

were built. They lived somewhere below their peak and hiked daily to their posts. The guard at Winchester Mountain, for example, camped for several seasons at Twin Lakes before the CCC built a cabin on the peak.

These fire guards had a lonely and rugged duty. They would generally arrive at their posts in late June and depart in late August, though this might vary with weather conditions. Sometimes they arrived before the snow was out; the trail to Winchester Mountain was regularly blocked by snow until the middle of July. When this was the case, the lookout had to trudge up and down the mountain, transporting supplies in small amounts on his or her back until the packer and his horses could get through. Marian Enyeart, a lookout on Winchester Mountain in the 1950s, described her 12-by-12-foot home:

> The cabin was furnished with a bunk, stove, table, a few cupboards, a stool with glass insulators on the legs, a washtub, a leaky dishpan, a bucket and some pots, pans and utensils (usually rusty), a mop, and a broom with no handle. There was a Coleman gas lantern, a kerosene lamp, some tools, a shovel and an ax, and a water-can-back-pack, with a spray pump to use for fire suppression.[3]

The lookout life was quiet most of the time. Occasionally there would be a long spell of dry weather, when fire danger would rise very high; sharp

Forest Service packtrain leaving Glacier

Austin Pass Ski Shelter under CCC construction, 1940

and constant attention was necessary during such periods. At other times the fog and rain would close in, completely obscuring visibility, sometimes for days or even weeks, and there was nothing to do but huddle in sweaters and sleeping bag with a book or other entertainment. The stove did little to chase the damp chill of such times, and fuel was always scarce. Rare lightning storms provided some excitement. The lookout then perched on the insulated stool, spotting and locating every lightning strike. When the storm passed, the lookout would continue to watch these strikes and report any smoke to Glacier by telephone, if the line had not gone down in the storm. The lookouts in the Glacier District could communicate with each other and District Headquarters in Glacier through a switchboard at the Silver Fir Guard Station near Shuksan. They called in on a regular schedule, their primary contact with the outside world except for the occasional hiker or packer who visited their scenic perches. A lonely life, but the scenery was grand; many lookouts returned for duty year after year.

As the 1930s drew to a close, recreational use of the Mount Baker region continued to increase. The Mount Baker Development Company continued its operation at Heather Meadows. The road was open all year, and several major ski meets were held. The Forest Service reported that recreational visitors to the Mount Baker National Forest as a whole had been an estimated 27,498 in 1924 with no recorded winter sports. Fifteen years later the total was an estimated 132,000; 48,500 of these were winter visitors.[4] Nearly all winter visits were recorded at Heather Meadows. This was significant growth; promoters and developers were hopeful of a prosperous future, but world events once again affected their aspirations and plans.

When the United States entered World War II late in 1941, people suddenly had far less time and money for outdoor recreation. Gasoline shortages made it impossible for the Highway Department to keep the road to Heather Meadows open. With no income generated the Development Com-

Slalom race, 1930s

Heather Inn

pany went bankrupt; its property was sold at a sheriff's sale. During the war the facilities at Heather Meadows, both those in private and Forest Service hands, were virtually abandoned. Occasional parties from the Mount Baker Ski Club still visited the Meadows, but winter silence returned to the area.

The Forest Service continued its fire surveillance, bolstered in 1942 by an Aircraft Warning Service run by the Army with Forest Service cooperation. A system of twenty-four observation posts were activated in the Glacier District, and sixty employees were added. This system operated until the winter of 1943, when diminishing threats of a Japanese air attack and heavy snow drove the observers from their stations.

Mount Baker Club activities were also curtailed during the war. Many club members went into the service. Skiing accounts, which had dominated club records in the 1930s, dwindled during the war. The ski cabin and Kulshan Cabin fell into disrepair. A few hiking groups ventured into the high country during the summers of the period, but human activity on and around Mount Baker was the least since 1891.

After the war, people came back to the mountains. A new company was formed to revive the resort; the buildings at Heather Meadows were repaired and reopened; and in the spring of 1946 the Bagley rope tow was restarted. Climbers returned to Mount Baker in search of ever more difficult challenges. The Mount Baker Club continued its visits, now primarily a hiking club. And the Forest Service dedicated itself increasingly to the harvest of the rich timber resources of the area.

There was still no road up Glacier Creek in 1946. Nor was there a road very far up the valley of the Middle Fork of the Nooksack. The country around the mountain remained largely wild and pristine. In the late 1940s the Forest Service decided it was time to open the extensive timber resources of Glacier Creek, and the Seaboard Logging Company built a road and began cutting timber. As the decade drew to a close, the road reached to within two miles of Kulshan Cabin. The cabin had not been maintained during the 1940s, and it was in bad shape. Consequently, when the Glacier Creek Road opened for public use, the Mount Baker Club and Western Washington State College, who jointly maintained the cabin, decided that a new building was necessary. They removed the old one in 1951 and built another close by the original site. Climbers and hikers would still have a destination and shelter high on the slopes of Mount Baker.

The post-war period saw a new breed of mountaineer. These climbers would not be content to simply follow the standard routes up the mountain pioneered earlier in the century by a generation of mountaineers using relatively primitive equipment and technique. The post-war climbers would come to the Pacific Northwest's great peaks with a thirst for bold and difficult ways to the summits. They would find them.

10

Modern Mountaineering

---

*It is the positive force that requires a man to go forward even
when every muscle rebels. It is man against the mountain—
finite man against the universe.*

*In these moments man discovers himself: what the limits of
his endurance are, how far the spirit will enable him to go.
Then he discovers the power of his soul to carry him on.*
— William O. Douglas, 1950

Edmund Coleman sought the line of least resistance to Mount
Baker's summit. Merely getting up there was challenge
enough for him. His distinction was that he was first. After Coleman, however, simply reaching the top was not challenge
enough. Climbers sought new and unexplored ways up the
mountain. Over the years they found many ways to climb its
south, east and northeast slopes. The unclimbed north and northwest walls looked simply impassable.

The steepest slopes of the mountain are these walls. The
north face is bordered on the south by a rotten volcanic ridge
called the Roman Nose, on the northeast by the long Cockscomb
Ridge. The face is split by North Ridge, the upper part of which is
capped by part of Roosevelt Glacier. The entire face is imposing.
Coleman Headwall, lying between the Roman Nose and North
Ridge, consists of steep ice and unstable rock. Roosevelt Headwall, on the other side of North Ridge, is a steep and heavily
crevassed glacier. Eighty years passed after Coleman's first ascent
before anyone climbed this face, Mount Baker's "Nordwand."

The key figure in the exploration of this side of the mountain
was Fred Beckey. Raised in the Northwest, he was drawn to the

mountains at the age of thirteen. The Boy Scouts and The Mountaineers gave him his start and basic techniques, and before long Beckey was emerging as one of the outstanding young climbers in America. He first came to Mount Baker in 1939 and followed Joe Morovits' footsteps up Boulder Glacier. In March of 1947 he returned to the mountain and climbed it on skis. The unclimbed Nordwand beckoned him, but a busy season in the British Columbia Coast Mountains precluded a return until the summer of 1948.

The face was still untouched when Beckey, with cousins Ralph and Dick Widrig, approached the mountain up the newly built logging road that had superseded Glacier Creek Trail to within two miles of Kulshan Cabin. After a night in the cabin, the three men threaded their way through the crevasses of Coleman Glacier to the base of the North Ridge. The lower part of the ridge required step-kicking; as the slope gradually steepened the trio put on their crampons. They made steady upward progress, slowly approaching the ice cliff that caps the ridge at 9,600 feet, the most difficult part of the climb. In his account of his North Cascade climbing exploits, *Challenge of the North Cascades*, Beckey describes how the difficulties were overcome.

Fatigue had made the ice wall seem impossibly distant, though in fact only a few hundred feet above. Soon we saw that to outflank the worst parts we would have to climb its left edge, where the ridge narrows quite sharply. The wall on the right is shorter but more vertical; the ridge, rising at an angle varying between 50° and 65° looked more feasible.

...to the left we stared down the longest ice slopes we had seen that summer, and to the right the wall fell away to a steep cliff of rotten lava and black ice. Where the angle increased above 45° Ralph chopped a large stance in the ice, and when he had his belay ready I began chopping a line up the steep ridge.... For two arduous hours I chopped, maintaining a delicate, strained balance on chipped-out handholds. On the second lead, though, we had a bit of luck: a curious small ice cavern large enough for a cold sitting belay. Ralph did all the shivering belaying of those 2 hours; Dick came last, hacking out the pitons as he climbed. Above the wall the slope angle decreased, but hopes for fast, non-belayed progress were premature. The crest became blue ice covered with loose snow and filmy crusts so variable in depth we could not trust ice ax belays. We were forced to excavate large stances for body belays, and to scrape away loose material before cutting a step. But despite all problems the ridge was exhilarating, a celestial pathway with only blue sky above. The covering on the ice became thicker; it was a relief to reach a wall of compact nevé. The interminable slope suddenly eased off and we stood on

Fred Beckey

a nearly level ridge crest with the summit visible only a few hundred feet above. A giant bergschrund blocked passage directly ahead to the summit dome, so we made a traverse left between large crevasses toward the exact summit, a little pumice mound peeping through the ice. Ten hours had elapsed since we left the cabin.[1]

The wall so many climbers had decided was beyond them had yielded in almost routine fashion. The climb had been straightforward except for the ice cliff; it would become a popular moderate route for modern climbers with improved equipment and technique.

Beckey could see good routes on the glacial headwalls on both sides of North Ridge and intended to be the first to climb them. Coleman Glacier Headwall was climbed, however, before he could get to it. This headwall rises from about 8,300 to 10,500 feet, with over 2,000 feet of climbing on slopes averaging forty-five degrees. It consists of a series of short ice cliffs bordered by the Roman Nose on the south and a rock face and ice rim on the northeast. The face is raked at times by falling ice and rock.

On August 18, 1957, Phil Bartow, Ed Cooper, Don Grimlund and Dave Nicholson made the first climb of this headwall. They approached the climb

Climber near steam vents on Mount Baker

across Coleman Glacier and started up an avalanche cone that lay at the foot of the face between two rock islands. They encountered difficulties immediately, for a crevasse blocked their path, forcing them to traverse to the right on hard, steep snow toward the rock island. When they could turn upward again, they had to climb a steep pitch of ice, followed by two hundred feet of moderate climbing.

After this stretch of relatively easy going, the climbing again became difficult. Cooper describes it:

> After some 60' of 60° slopes, one man finally reached a belay spot with standing-room only in a crevasse. The knife edge ridge of the lower lip of the crevasse was traversed to a point where the two lips joined, and Bartow surmounted a 5' near vertical section.[2]

This steep step behind them, they worked their way up several hundred feet of forty-five-to-fifty-degree snow slopes until they found themselves beneath the upper ice cliffs. Moving to the right, they climbed through these obstacles where two large crevasses bisect the upper portion of the face. Several hundred feet of steep climbing along a narrow rock outcropping brought them to the point where the angle of the face eased off to the summit plateau. Almost twelve hours of strenuous climbing enabled them to make the first ascent of Coleman Headwall.

A prize coveted by Beckey had gone to someone else, but just barely. His busy climbing schedule brought him to the mountain to do this very climb only a few weeks later. Roosevelt Headwall remained to be done, so he put it on his schedule for the following year.

Before Beckey returned, two Canadian climbers did a variation on the Coleman Headwall route. In May, 1958, Henryk Mather and Les MacDonald of Vancouver, B.C., started up the avalanche cone as their predecessors had. Instead of veering to the right, though, they went directly up the face. In doing so they had to negotiate some very dangerous and loose ice rubble. At one point they were blocked by a rock and ice pillar but climbed around it on very steep ice and continued straight up it until they could penetrate the ice cliffs of the summit cap.[3] This was a more dangerous and difficult way up the headwall and pushed the challenge of climbing Mount Baker to yet another level of difficulty.

Fred Beckey came back in June, this time with Don Gordon and John Rupley. Their objective was the Roosevelt Glacier Headwall. This steep, heavily crevassed and avalanche-prone glacier is bordered on the south by North Ridge, on the northeast by Cockscomb Ridge. Beckey, Gordon and Rupley traversed across from Coleman Glacier, then started upward. Threading among the crevasses, they traversed left, or eastward, and up the left side of the glacier. It steepened at about 9,500 feet; they climbed a corridor between crevasses and up moderately steep firn and ice until they reached the lower lip of the great upper bergschrund, which slashes across the entire upper face. Avalanche debris provided a bridge across this huge crevasse. Then they climbed the nearly vertical ice of its upper lip using ice pitons for safety. After this they traversed diagonally leftward until they reached the upper part of Cockscomb Ridge, which they climbed to the summit.

Three major features of the Nordwand had been climbed. Its two containing features—Cockscomb Ridge and the Roman Nose—remained to be done. Both yielded to climbers in 1960.

Ed Cooper was back in search of another first ascent in June. Two years before he had climbed the mountain with his eye on the Roman Nose but had been intimidated by the rotten rock. He had climbed a new route on Colfax Peak, the eastern Black Butte that rises across Coleman Glacier from the Nose. He came back to try the Nose again, accompanied by Gordon Thompson, Mike Swayne and Don Ihlenfeldt. The party hiked to the base of the two-thousand-foot snakelike cleaver and found a snow finger that gave access to its crest of mud-lava. "After several discouraging leads," wrote Cooper, "we found that we could traverse on 45-60° snow just below and east of the ridge crest." This was greatly preferable to the rotten rock of the cleaver. They worked upward this way for a thousand feet and came to a vertical step in the ridge. This forced them to the right on a series of ledges, where they encountered black ice and had to chop steps. Surmounting the steep icy section, they continued upward on rotten rock until they reached yet another steep step. "While pitons would have been desirable, they were impossible to fix," noted Cooper.[5] Largely without protection, the four men again traversed to the right, this time in deep, wet snow over black ice. Two hundred feet of this insecure work brought them to a short rock pitch inundated with meltwater; they climbed up the pitch onto the ridge crest. The rock ridge gradually merged with a snow ridge, which they then followed, much relieved to be on relatively firm ground, onto the summit plateau.

Cooper's account of this climb gives the distinct impression that it was an unpleasant and dangerous venture. The party faced and met severe challenges—exciting, but conditions on the ridge were far from ideal. The climb was dangerous throughout because of the poor rock and lack of protection. A winter ascent of the route was made in January 1977 by Anton Karuza and Greg Thompson. With the mud-lava solidly frozen, they climbed more directly and with more security. They were able to climb chimneys and cracks, using nuts for protection, and avoid the traverses that the rotten rock forced upon the first ascent party. Their climb was challenging and enjoyable, and conditions were good. Weather was quite stable, and there was very little snow. Ordinarily, winter climbing on the mountain is difficult, but the unusually dry winter of 1977 gave Karuza and Thompson a great opportunity.

Cockscomb Ridge, which had frustrated so many aspirants beginning

Attaching crampons in preparation for Mount Baker climb. Triconi nailed boots were standard equipment for 1940s climbers.

with Dorr and his partner in 1882, was also finally climbed in 1960.[6] Parties had come up to the crumbly rock protruberance at 9,500 feet from various directions—Dorr and others up from Skyline Divide and Chowder Ridge; Morovits, the Mazamas and others from Ptarmigan Ridge and Park Glacier on the east—but no one had come up the ridge, negotiated the Cockscomb (earlier called "Pumice-Stone Pinnacle") and continued up the ridge to the summit—until Chuck Morley, John Musser and Klindt Vielbig did so on July 4, 1960.

The three approached the problem across Coleman and Roosevelt glaciers from Kulshan Cabin and climbed onto the ridge at the 7,800-foot level. From there they ascended the gradually steepening ridge, encountering tricky crevasses at nine thousand feet. A cliff of crumbly rock dropped steeply down to the Roosevelt Glacier on their right. A steep and crevassed tongue of Mazama Glacier sloped down to the left. Thin snow bridges

Climber on left gives ice axe belay to leader, crossing an ice bridge.

enabled them to cross the crevasses, but they were then forced to make a long contour to the left, or east, in order to get around the bergschrund at the head of Mazama Glacier. Snow slopes led to mud-lava, and they finally reached the ridge crest and the Cockscomb.

At this point they were benighted and bivouacked just below their major problem. Next morning they tackled the "tower," which "was gained in the most direct line by steep snow on the east side."[7] It was utterly impossible to climb on the rock of the pinnacle itself, for it is extremely crumbly volcanic material (at one time the pinnacle was a double formation, but one of the two pillars fell away onto Roosevelt Glacier). The three climbers stayed as high as they could in order to lay claim to a direct ascent of the ridge. As they traversed past the three-hundred-foot pinnacle they were on extremely steep snow, but they made the passage without mishap, regained the crest of the ridge and continued on to the top. Modern technique and snow- and ice-climbing equipment rendered the success that had eluded earlier aspirants. Mountaineering had come a long way since Joe Morovits initially probed the area for a route, equipped only with his hobnail boots and rifle.

The major routes on Mount Baker itself had been climbed, but there were other fields in the area for climbers in search of firsts. As noted earlier, Ed Cooper and Fergus O'Conner came to the mountain in early May of 1958 intent on climbing the Roman Nose, only to give up the idea because the good early season conditions they were hoping for were denied them. Instead, they turned their attention to the unclimbed ice wall rising between the lower and the main East Peak of Black Butte. The climb is known as the North Face route of Colfax Peak, and Cooper and O'Conner found it steep but surprisingly easy, thanks to unusual conditions. Huge ice blocks had avalanched off the glacier high on the peak, as they regularly do, but these blocks, instead of roaring down onto Coleman Glacier in their normal fashion, had lodged in the bergschrund and formed a bridge. Snow covered the bridge, and the two were able to climb over it and up through the gap left by the falling ice in the overhanging ice cliff. The climbers went up a steep ramp in snow soft enough for "excellent buckets"[8] and had their first ascent.

The other major summit of the Black Buttes, 9,096-foot Lincoln Peak had, two years earlier, proved a more challenging climb. Early in the morning of July 27, 1956, Fred Beckey, Wes Grande, John Rupley and Herb Staley set out from Kulshan Cabin intent on the first ascent of Lincoln Peak. They climbed Heliotrope Ridge, from which they gazed across the 1,500-foot-deep chasm of Thunder Glacier at their objective. They paused a while to ponder the desirable prospect of "basking amid lupine and fireweed for the day."[9] But ambition triumphed over lassitude, and they were soon sliding down to the glacier. They traversed below its snout and then beneath the western face of the butte.

Examining the southern face rising steeply above them, the four men found that it "presented a vast forest of lava rock in various stages of de-

View from a large crevasse

cay."[10] Its apron was a steep glacier, above which was a maze of gullies topped by four towers. They climbed the glacier, negotiated the moat above it and started up the largest gully toward the second tower from the left. As they climbed, the "hollow echo of falling rock above revealed the presence of an anti-social billy goat within 300 feet of our summit choice."[11]

The men abandoned most of their climbing hardware, thinking that if a goat could do the climb they certainly could follow without much technical difficulty. Up the gully they went for a thousand feet on loose snow and rock lying at a steep fifty-five degree angle, and by 1 p.m. they were looking over a col above the north face. From here they turned to the left, or westward, 150 feet below their summit tower. Clouds blanketed the mountain and valleys below, though they could occasionally look through "veiled windows"[12] at climbers on the Coleman Glacier.

The next 150 feet of work required great care, for they climbed over loose blocks, then up a rotten forty-foot chimney that required stemming, and an exposed, narrow crack. Finally reaching the top of their tower, the four gazed in frustration across at the true summit eighty feet higher. Not about to quit short of the top, they rapelled into the forty-foot gap separating the towers, fixed a rope for the return trip and climbed to the summit. "At approximately 3 p.m., well chilled and cheated of a view, we emptied a sardine can as a register and affixed a jaunty red ribbon to the cairn."[13] After a dangerous descent they returned to their camp fifteen hours after leaving it. Herb Staley summed it up: "Basically, the climb is a problem in route-finding, but the attendant hazards more than compensate for any lack of technical difficulty. None of us would care to repeat the climb or to recommend it."[14]

The search for "firsts" on the mountain continues to the present, but there are few to report from recent years. Several variations on established routes have been done. In 1961 a party climbed Easton Glacier to a notch at 9,600 feet on Easton-Talum Cleaver. Instead of climbing westward up Baker's main peak as other parties had done (beginning with the 1909 Mazama climb), they descended into the crater. The group explored a bit, examining steam vents and the crater outlet onto Boulder Glacier, then climbed Boulder Glacier northward to the summit.

In 1970 a party forged a new route up Park Glacier Headwall, climbing directly up its middle. The upper part of the climb was steep and difficult, involving negotiation of a bergschrund and cornice. A party of five from Oregon did a new variation up the Roosevelt Glacier that same year. And in January of 1977 the first winter ascent of the Roman Nose was completed.

In the nearly one hundred and twenty years that people have been climbing Mount Baker, many thousands have attempted the ascent. The sport of mountaineering has exploded in popularity in recent years, and the "majors," the dominant volcanoes of the Cascades, have been among the most coveted objectives. Indeed, so many climbers traipse up the Coleman-Deming Glacier route at the peak of the season that they wear a trench in the snow visible to the naked eye twenty miles away. The exploits of the multitudes may not be newsworthy, but they are of great personal significance to the climbers themselves. A few climbers in the history of the mountain stand out: Coleman, Morovits, Lee, Beckey and Cooper among them. These men were all pioneers, overcoming barriers and exploring new ground and new possibilities. The opportunities for exploration will not come again. The climbs of Mount Baker's Nordwand mark the end of an era in climbing on the mountain. Great climbs displaying high skill and daring continue to occur, but the only "pioneering" that remains involves winter ascents of the more demanding routes. The element of uncertainty that gives such excitement to being first to explore any part of the earth seems no longer possible.

11

Accidents and Rescues

When man knows how to live dangerously, he is not afraid to die.
When he is not afraid to die, he is, strangely, free to live.
—William O. Douglas, 1950

F ear gripped Edmund T. Coleman on that day in 1868 when he,
Tennant and Ogilvy watched Thomas Stratton stride confidently across the glacier without benefit of rope or companion.
He knew, as perhaps Stratton did not, what perils lurked on the
ice for the unprepared. The principal threat to Stratton was the
hidden crevasse. A smooth, seemingly innocent expanse of snow
could be a death trap, sections of it merely inches thick where
winter snow melting from the surface downward remains a thin
bridge over a crack that may be a hundred feet deep. If Stratton
happened to step in such a place, down he would go, perhaps to
fatal injury in the fall, perhaps to a slower death from hypothermia in the icy cavern. What bothered Coleman and many experienced climbers since was not only the danger to Stratton, but its
avoidability. His party had laboriously carried ropes up the
mountain to minimize the threat of a glacial plunge.

Stratton's enthusiasm was not his undoing, but others over
the years have not been as fortunate. Mount Baker has, as some
would say, been a "killer." Eighteen people have died on the
mountain since Coleman's initial climb. Many others have been
injured. Still others have had narrow escapes. Mishaps have also
occurred on other mountains in the region. People came to take
the risks of the high mountains casually, an attitude that reached
its peak with the marathons. The races dramatized the dangers so
that such casualness was reduced, but it has always been present

C.C. Wright (left) and J.C. Bishop

to some degree, with unhappy results.

Is it correct to say that Mount Baker is a killer? Such a view imputes malicious intent to an inanimate mound of rock and ice. The story of accidents and tragedies on any mountain is one of "objective" dangers—the fall of rocks, ice or snow, the occurrence of sudden storms—and "subjective" dangers, those created by the mental and physical conditions of climbers, their judgment, training, preparation and skill. Some accidents might have been avoided by a more fit and experienced person; some could not because circumstances brought a person and a falling block of ice together at a particular moment. In either case, the mountain is not responsible.

Many observers who themselves do not venture up onto the high mountains argue that the mistake leading to a mishap was made when the

Evacuation of J.C. Bishop, 1913

person traveled up into the area of risk. If someone knows there is a risk, these observers contend, then the reasonable thing to do is avoid the situation entirely. They cannot fathom why anyone would voluntarily put themselves at risk. The entire story of Mount Baker exploration, of all mountaineering, is that of people seeking a challenge. Flirting with danger, mastering a situation full of hazards is a thrilling and fulfilling experience for many people. The rewards balance the potential costs. The compensation is spiritual and personal, not material. And there always seem to be people seeking such intangibles. Climbers have calculated the risks of Mount Baker, gambled with the odds and have won or lost.

Early Mount Baker climbers had close calls. On his second attempt Coleman was forced to bivouac high on the mountain, as were Glisan and Lee and later Easton and his companions. They performed well, luck was with them and they escaped without injury. The first death related to mountaineering (Dick Smith's death by his own rifle excepted) was that of J.C. Bishop in July of 1913. Bishop was an experienced mountaineer who had been the first President of the British Columbia Mountaineering Club, an office he held for three years. He was climbing Mount Baker to warm up for an extended venture into the Canadian Rockies. C.C. Wright, an early resident of Glacier, was climbing with him when the accident occurred. The two had climbed to the summit and were descending Roosevelt Glacier (the part of the glacier where the mishap occurred later was found to be a separate glacier and was named for Coleman) when Bishop plunged into a hidden crevasse. Some accounts claim he inadvertently stepped backward into the crevasse while taking a picture. Regardless of what caused his fall, Bishop became wedged head first down into the narrow bottom of the crevasse. Wright, who barely escaped falling in himself, was unable to extricate him. Bishop may have died from the fall or from hypothermia; the record is unclear. Wright rushed down the mountain for help, but Bishop was dead long before the rescuers reached him.

Bishop's accident occurred just before the running of the third Mount Baker Marathon. Little note of the incident appeared in Bellingham newspapers, perhaps because the victim was not a local man, perhaps because boosters were concerned that it might cast a cloud over the race or even result in its cancellation. By 1913 some people were concerned enough to publicly question the wisdom of the race. Despite Bishop's death, however, the third race was held, and Victor Galbraith nearly met the same fate. Luck was with him, but the two incidents provided dramatic evidence of the dangers of climbing the mountain, and the marathon was ended. Efforts were made to revive the marathon in later years, but each time the hazards cited were sufficient reason not to do so.

Twenty-six years passed before another fatal accident occurred on the mountain. Many climbers ventured up, but most did so in highly organized groups. The safety-consciousness of the time was reflected in the Mount Baker Club's newsletter. It stated unequivocably that the club was opposed to stunt climbers, who went on climbs without proper guides and organization. Further, the club disapproved of climbs in which less than three persons participated. These admonitions may have been prompted by the small parties that were venturing onto Baker in the late 1920s, principally from northeast of the mountain, where the Mount Baker Lodge was in full swing.

The next fatal accident, and the worst tragedy to occur in Mount Baker's climbing history, befell a large and well-organized party complete with competent guides. Since 1917, college students and faculty from Western Washington College of Education in Bellingham (now Western Washington University) had made an annual outing to the mountain. They had come in large groups, climbing the mountain each year, and had never encountered any problems. They had always traveled up the Glacier Trail to Kulshan Cabin and made the ascent up Coleman Glacier to the saddle, then up the upper Deming Glacier to the summit. Members were given instruction in the use of ice axes and proper procedures for safe climbing. Their preparation had always proven sufficient.

On Saturday, July 22, 1939, twenty-five climbers from the college began their ascent before dawn, according to normal procedure. Two Mount

Baker veterans were leading. Don Coss was guide and Chet Ullin was his assistant. All went well as the party made its way over Coleman Glacier.
Storms had dumped new snow on the higher reaches of the peak, but it had
settled and seemed to offer no problems. Such storms are normal any time of
the year on the upper mountain, and on the day of the climb the weather
was clear and beautiful.

As the morning wore on, the sun shone brightly and people stripped
off jackets and sweaters because of the heat. Everyone was climbing well;
the party had reached the last steep section of the upper Deming Glacier.
They were perhaps fifteen minutes from the summit plateau, spread out in
single file climbing straight up the steep slope, when their exultation turned
to terror.

> All of a sudden there was a swishing sound and a fine layer of
> loose snow began to sluff off the steep slope, gaining in thickness
> as it continued. The party was at the upper end of the sliding
> snow and before they knew it the members found themselves all
> sliding with it as though they were standing on a moving carpet.
> Some of them lost their balance right away and a shout went out
> from one of the guides to "Dig in!" This they did only to find that
> when they sunk their alpenstocks and ice axes into the moving
> snow, the force of the slide bent them over from the firm snow
> underneath as though they were blades of grass. Some swam,
> some crawled, but all of them were down, then up again, all fight-
> ing to move upwards so the sliding snow would all finally pass
> underneath them.[1]

The entire party of twenty-five were carried hundreds of feet down the
slope until the slide stopped. Everyone was dazed. The guides, keeping their
heads, made a count of the group. Six were missing. They ordered the group
to traverse off the glacier to the saddle. Ullin and Coss then went in search of
the missing climbers.

While the two guides were searching for survivors, the rest of the party
waited in the saddle. They did not go out onto the glacier to search for their
missing companions because conditions at the terminus of the avalanche
were judged extremely dangerous. Small slides continued to come down the
slope, and Coss and Ullin feared that someone else would be injured. Everyone was deeply shaken and their judgment perhaps affected by their narrow
escape, so the two guides did their best.

The slide had finally stopped when it reached a crevassed area of
Deming Glacier, just below the level of the saddle. It had flowed over two ice
cliffs and gone into a huge crevasse. The two searchers worked among the
cliffs and crevasses for three hours, joined after a while by the two most experienced members of the climbing party. One woman was quickly rescued.

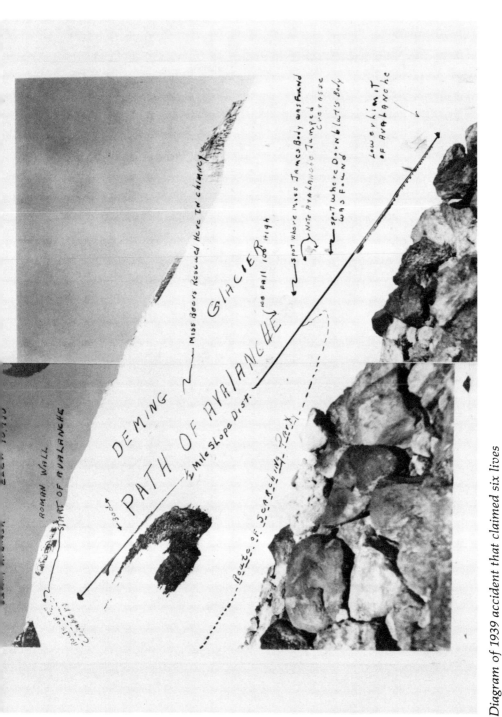

Diagram of 1939 accident that claimed six lives

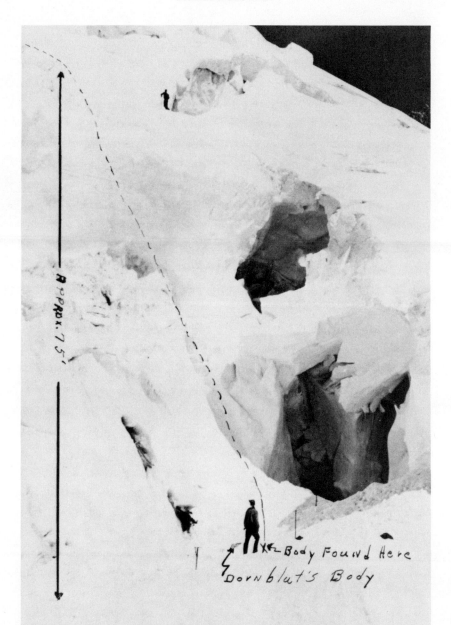

view of Lower CREVASSE INTO WHICH
Dornblut's Body Fell. Note Depth of Snow
Fall. Probably 40-50 Foot AVALANche snow
slid into This crevasse

A second was uncovered three hours after she had been buried. Ullin worked frantically to save her, giving her artificial respiration for one and a half hours, but could not revive her. Finally, as the afternoon waned and hope of finding anyone else alive diminished, the dejected and exhausted searchers gave up and set off down the mountain for Kulshan Cabin. Other head counts revealed that seven students had initially been missing. One had been rescued, one was known to be dead. Five were missing.

At 8 p.m. two members of the party reported the accident to District Ranger William Parke at the Glacier Ranger Station. He pulled together a rescue party which included himself, three other Forest Service employees and six CCC enrollees. They made the ten-mile hike to Kulshan Cabin with flashlights, arriving there at 3 a.m. Refreshed by a brief rest and breakfast, the rescue group, accompanied by Coss and Ullin, headed upward at 5:30. They reached the saddle and were examining the avalanche when three more volunteer searchers caught up with them. This brought the rescue group to a strength of fifteen.

Three people took the body of Alice James, uncovered the previous afternoon, down the mountain in an improvised canvas toboggan, and the twelve others entered the slide area and resumed probing and searching. Soon they found another body, that of Julius Dornblut, Jr., buried under three feet of snow. It had passed through a chute between seracs, dropped a hundred feet over an ice wall and gone seventy feet into a crevasse. Dornblut's location confirmed the fears of the searchers that the other missing students were probably buried deep in the large crevasse.

They worked through the day but found no one else, finally returning to Kulshan Cabin exhausted from their labors and sleepless night. The search went on for thirteen days but no more bodies were ever found. Deming Glacier is the final resting place for Hope Weitman, Beulah Lindberg, Maynard Howat and Vene Fisher.

There was much debate about whether this accident could have been avoided. Most informed people concluded that it could not. Midsummer snowstorms are common on the mountain; in Baker's entire climbing history there have been only two recorded incidents like this one. (The other was a fatality in the same place in late summer of 1979.) Coss and Ullin judged the snow stable enough to travel on. Perhaps they did not expect the temperature to be quite as warm as it turned out to be, with the summer sun beating directly onto the steep slope and its fresh snow. The party was large, and it may have climbed more slowly than it should have. Hindsight raises many factors that contributed to the tragedy. At the time and "on the ground" the guides saw no cause for alarm and were following established procedures on a commonly climbed route. Circumstances conspired to bring down the unusually large avalanche far enough to bury the unfortunate students.

Five years after the college group's mishap, another fatality occurred in

August, 1944. Two young members of The Mountaineers from Seattle were doing their summer "tour" of the mountains. Larry Strathdee and Jack Schwabland, ages sixteen and seventeen, climbed Glacier Peak and then came up to Mount Baker. Confident of good weather and a speedy ascent, they hiked the trail to Boulder Ridge with light packs, leaving even their sleeping bags in their car.

The climb up the ridge and glacier went smoothly, and at noon they neared the summit. Here they were faced with an option—they could stay on the glacier and climb easily onto the summit, or they could go up a steep slope of ice above the bergschrund, which would lead them to crumbly rock cliffs up which they could climb to the top. Larry insisted that they should go the hard way. Jack was not for the idea. Finally Jack simply refused to go up the ice slope, so Larry set out to do it alone. Climbing unroped and not even bothering to cut steps, Larry lost his footing and began to slide down the ice sheet toward the bergschrund. He was unable to slow his slide with his ice axe, overshot the schrund and landed on the lower lip, a fall of fifty feet. He slid another two hundred feet down steep ice before he finally stopped.

Jack traversed over to his badly injured companion. They were in a fix. Help was a long way off. There was no sleeping bag to protect Larry from hypothermia. There was no one to attend the injured man while Jack went for help. Jack did what he could, giving him all the clothing he could spare and making him as comfortable as possible, but could not move him off the glacier.

Jack raced down the mountain, reaching the ranger station near Baker Lake at 8 p.m. A rescue party was organized, but it was late the next afternoon before it reached the scene of the accident. Larry was dead from a combination of head injuries, shock and hypothermia. Mount Baker had claimed the life of one who took it too lightly.

Eighteen years passed before another fatal accident occurred; hundreds of people safely climbed the mountain during those years. Then in November of 1962, Hans Jorritsma, a South African, and Joan Huckell of Sydney, Australia, approached the mountain along Ptarmigan Ridge, bent on climbing up Park Glacier. Huckell apparently was not up to the climb, so Jorritsma left her on or near Rainbow Glacier, a rather flat, small glacier near the northeastern base of the peak. He proceeded alone, climbing above the Cockscomb to a point some two hundred feet below the summit. The weather was excellent, but November days are short. He turned back just below the summit for lack of time. He had not been able to climb rapidly, for he had no crampons and was forced to cut many steps in his ascent of the headwall of Park Glacier.

Jorritsma descended and joined Huckell. They roped up and proceeded toward the Portals, a formation of rock pinnacles that flanks an access route onto Rainbow Glacier. Somewhere near the West Portal Jorritsma slipped and pulled Huckell down with him. The two slid a short distance, the woman striking some rocks and receiving head and chest injuries. Her breathing was difficult. She could barely walk, so Jorritsma helped her to the edge of the glacier and made a temporary camp in a moat.

The accident occurred at about 3 p.m. Jorritsma stayed with Huckell until 3 a.m., when he finally decided to go for help. Instead of going back out Ptarmigan Ridge to the Mount Baker Ski Area, Jorritsma took what he thought was a shortcut directly down Wells Creek. This route was much longer than he thought, and it was many hours before he finally reached the Mount Baker Highway where he got a ride to the Glacier Ranger Station.

Perhaps suffering from shock himself, the exhausted climber reported that the injured woman was on the trail. Thinking that this meant rescuers might reach her in the remaining daylight, the Forest Service enlisted the help of Dr. Otto Trott, a veteran climber who was working on his cabin near Glacier, and thirteen Marine reservists who were in the area on a training exercise. The sixteen men (one Forest Service man and Jorritsma went along) drove to trailhead near Table Mountain, and set out along Ptarmigan Ridge.

The weather had changed dramatically. Heavy snow was falling and high winds battered the exposed ridge. The rescue party reached Camp Kiser, just beyond which the trail ends, and found that they were still a long way from the injured woman. The Marines were dressed in cotton pants and long parkas, and no one in the party was prepared to spend a night exposed to such severe weather. They had no choice but to retreat to a stand of trees, build a fire and tend to their own survival.

At daylight the storm still raged as they set out again and were overtaken by a rescue team from the Seattle Mountain Rescue Council. This augmented group still had trouble finding Huckell. Visibility was very poor, and Jorritsma had trouble locating the spot where he had left her. Finally at noon, two nights and forty-five hours after the accident, they reached the bivouac site. Huckell was dead, her body covered with one and a half feet of new snow. Conditions were too severe to remove her body, so the team left it there intending to come back for it soon. But a series of storms buried the area. It was not until the following July that a Bellingham Mountain Rescue team was able to retrieve the remains of the unfortunate woman.

Another tragic incident occurred in 1969. On May 25 four young Canadians were skiing on Coleman Glacier, as many people do in late spring and early summer. Ski areas were closed for the season, but these dedicated skiers put "skins" on their skis and walked up as far as they wished to enjoy challenging runs. Each year a few experts climb to the very summit and ski down, confidently (some would say foolishly) negotiating their way among the crevasses.

The four young skiers in this case reached the saddle and decided to climb to the summit before their run down. Leaving their skis and packs just above the saddle, they took their ski poles and started upward, climbing in their ski boots. The weather changed rapidly. On the descent from the summit the entire group, roped together, slid seventy-five to a hundred feet and then dropped over a twenty-five-foot rock cliff. John Dallmeyer, the only member of the party with any climbing experience, was killed. Judy Small was injured. Mario Strim and Margaret Secrett survived the fall unscathed.

Strim and Secrett dug a snow hole, probably with their hands, and placed the injured woman in it to shield her from the icy wind. They then huddled together nearby, struggling for warmth as a storm raged on the mountain. By next morning all were dead, Small from a combination of trauma and hypothermia, the other two from hypothermia. The group was reported missing, but because of the storm it was several days before the rescue teams were able to reach the scene of the accident.

Here was a disaster caused by subjective factors. Certainly a storm blew in, but had the party set off downward immediately, they probably would have escaped. Their climbing equipment was inadequate, though many climb to the summit similarly ill-equipped with no problems. Ski poles are no substitute for ice axes in arresting a fall. Most disastrously, they ventured upward in the gathering storm without adequate clothing or emergency equipment. The group started its outing in deceptively warm and sunny conditions and was surprised when the weather changed quickly and drastically. Many parties reach the summit poorly prepared but are lucky enough to have good weather. These four were not so lucky.

There have been other serious accidents and fatalities. A University of Washington student died in 1973 when, inadequately dressed, he became hypothermic on a climb of the Coleman Headwall. The summer of 1979 was a disastrous one. A single crevasse claimed two lives in separate accidents, and in August a fatality occurred on Deming Glacier in a situation much like that of the 1939 avalanche disaster. Mountain rescue teams were on the mountain weekly from mid-July through August. The most recent fatality occurred on New Year's Day, 1981, in a skiing accident. Conditions were extremely icy; one woman died and two men were seriously injured on an outing near Kulshan Cabin.

There is another side to the story of death and injury on Mount Baker. All mishaps do not, of course, end in the death of the victim. People often are rescued—by their own party, by other climbers or by rescue teams. Rescues far outnumber the fatalities, and there have been some dramatic, even heroic, efforts over the years. It is testimony to the skill and perseverance of the rescuers that only eighteen lives have been lost in over a century of intensive human endeavor on the mountain.

One rescue, in October of 1979, had all of the elements of a well-oiled rescue operation on a big, glaciated Northwest mountain. The story begins when experienced climbers descending Coleman Glacier encountered a pair of young novice climbers camped below the Black Buttes. The two young men proudly said that they were going to climb the Coleman Headwall;

they would not be dissuaded by the more experienced men, who pointed out that it was not a beginner's climb any time of the year—in October it was a challenge even for experts. The climbers who spotted the youths were so concerned that when they came off the mountain they reported their encounter to the Whatcom County Sheriff, who coordinates all rescue work in the region. They believed that a serious problem might be imminent. This initial report was made late Saturday.

Sunday began as a nice day, but gradually the weather deteriorated. By nightfall a strong storm was blasting the mountain. Heavy rain and high winds buffeted the lowlands throughout the night and Monday, and snow fell on higher elevations. The two young climbers had signed in for the climb at the Glacier Ranger Station but had not signed out by Monday evening. The Saturday prediction was fulfilled, and a rescue operation was initiated. The decision to start the rescue machinery moving rests with the deputy sheriff in charge of search and rescue, who is advised by the Bellingham Mountain Rescue Council. The initial report of the potential problem, the bad weather and the climbers' failure to sign out gave ample reason to begin a rescue operation.

By dawn on Tuesday a team of rescuers stood on the moraine below Coleman Glacier sorting equipment. They were from the Bellingham and Seattle Mountain Rescue Councils and had traveled through the night to be ready to search at dawn. The weather was clear and very cold. Six inches of new snow lay over the rocks of the moraine and the rock-hard ice of the glacier. A cold wind blew snow across the ice, creating at times a knee-deep ground blizzard. Since the missing climbers could be anywhere on the mountain, the small force was to spread out in rope teams and work their way up Coleman Glacier to the base of the headwall, looking into crevasses as they went.

As the teams started up, the thud of helicopter rotors broke the wintery stillness. A large "bird" from the Whidbey Island Naval Air Station had picked up a Bellingham Mountain Rescue observer and was to inspect the headwall. As the rescuers on the ground ventured slowly onto the glacier, the chopper flew slowly back and forth across the face. The helicopter crew spotted the missing climbers' tent, or what was left of it after the storm. There was no sign of life around the camp, and they found nothing on the face. The aircraft dropped the observer off on the Glacier Creek road, and flew back to its base to refuel.

Meanwhile on the glacier, Al Errington and Joe Kasuba of Seattle Mountain Rescue examined several crevasses then sat down several feet from the lip of a large one for a rest and a snack. As they sat there, the snow under them suddenly cracked off and thundered into the crevasse, throwing the two backward forty feet down into the glacier. Errington righted himself. His back had been sprained in the fall, but no bones had been broken. He looked around for Joe in the jumble of ice blocks that had fallen into the crevasse but could only see the rope disappearing among them. At first he thought that Joe had been buried, perhaps crushed.

Fortunately, however, Joe had also landed on top of the debris but had been more seriously injured. Al soon found him, located the radio the two were carrying and called for help. All rescue teams abandoned the search for the missing climbers and converged on the crevasse. Al and Joe's fellow Seattle team members climbed into the crevasse to help with Joe's injuries; the Bellingham Mountain Rescue men tackled the problem of preparing for a helicopter evacuation of the victims.

The slope below the crevasse dropped off moderately to other crevasses 150 feet below. A slip down the slope would end in one of these crevasses, so great care had to be taken in moving around. A fixed rope was set up to allow safe movement along the lower lip of the crevasse where the rescuers were working. The helicopter returned from its refueling run and came up to the accident site. First it attempted to lower a medical corpsman but rescuers frantically waved the chopper away from the crevasse for fear that concussion of the rotor blades would knock more debris down. A huge block of snow and ice was wedged into the crevasse; a fairly easy evacuation could be made by traversing beneath this block to where the crevasse floor (actually a snow bridge) rose to the surface of the glacier. If the block collapsed it would not only endanger the rescuers, but would necessitate a much more complex procedure to raise the injured man to where he could be lifted by the helicopter. The corpsman, a member of the U.S. Navy helicopter crew, was lowered on the end of a steel cable to the hard icy slope west of the accident site. He had no crampons or ice axe, only his slick-soled boots. It was clear to rescuers on the ground that the moment he released himself from the cable he would slide down the slope into a crevasse. They waved their arms against the move (rescuers on the ground and in the chopper were on different radio frequencies and so could not communicate) and the pilot finally understood and took their advice. He flew away with the corpsman dangling on the end of the cable, which was jammed. The crew eventually managed to haul him back into the ship. The ice block stayed in place.

Again the helicopter came back, this time lowering a litter to several climbers who had anchored themselves to the mountainside well away from the crevasse. They caught the litter, dragged it across the steep slope to the crevasse, and Joe was placed in it. He was in great pain from multiple injuries, and his condition was becoming serious. The litter was gingerly moved along the crevasse, under the ice block and up to the glacier's surface. Again the chopper came up, the blast from its rotors creating a hurricane. The blowing snow made visibility almost nil. Despite these blizzard conditions, the cable was lowered and attached to the litter, and Joe was lifted off the glacier. As the machine hovered, a great thump could be heard and felt as the ice block collapsed into the crevasse. But everyone was by now well away from it, and the injured man was successfully raised into the helicopter and

Whidbey Island Naval Air helicopter lowers Bellingham Mountain Rescue crew onto glacier.

Bellingham Mountain Rescue member "tends" the litter being raised out of a large moat.

flown to the hospital in Bellingham. He recovered from his injuries.

There was still no sign of the original pair whom everyone had come to assist. The ground searchers came off the glacier, exhausted from the effort of saving one of their own, and the helicopter flew back over the mountain for more aerial searching. They found nothing. Volunteers driving the Middle Fork Road came upon the two exhausted youths.

Despite their inexperience, the two had successfully climbed the Coleman Headwall on Sunday in deteriorating weather. Their intention was to descend Deming Glacier and then Coleman Glacier to their tent, but in the blowing mist and snow they became confused and descended the eastern side of the mountain instead. They reached timberline as the full force of the storm hit the mountain, and they spent Sunday night there, wet and cold but sheltered. Instead of continuing on downward to Baker Lake, they tried to traverse back south and west around the mountain, undoubtedly intending to return to their tent. They endured two more nights before they finally were discovered—tired, cold and hungry but uninjured. Their navigation skills had failed them, but their survival skills had been exceptional.

The accident that befell the rescuers is a perfect example of an unavoidable objective occurrence. The tons of ice that broke off had probably been poised to do so for days. The two rescuers just happened to be there when it did. Perhaps their weight, though inconsequential in relation to the weight of the ice, tipped the balance. They had been placed in that spot by the miscalculations of the young climbers they were trying to rescue. Ironically, the experienced rescuers were hurt while the novices escaped injury. The two youths probably never gave the possibility of rescue a thought when plotting their adventure. Rescue teams seldom mind being called out to assist people who have been unlucky or who have erred, but this incident indicates what is at stake when a rescue is called for.

The story of every rescue on the mountain describes the hard reality of life and death. On Mount Baker, people rise to great heights, literally and figuratively, but they rise to a place where much of the safety and insulation of modern life has never reached. That is why they go up there—to encounter and struggle with the elements. Usually they win the struggle and are better for it. Sometimes they do not.

12

The Land of Many Uses

*National Parks should be relatively spacious land and
water areas so outstanding and superior in quality and beauty as
to make imperative their preservation by the Federal
Government for the enjoyment, education, and inspiration
of all people.*
— National Park Service pamphlet, 1972

The Mount Baker country has long been noted for the unsurpassed value of its natural resources. The mountain itself, with its glaciers and subalpine meadows, is of unexcelled scenic value. It is a dramatic scene, the dark green tree-covered slopes sweeping up through light green alpine meadows draped like a garment over the ridges, to the perpetually white dome of the mountain itself. Tall trees of great lumber value cover the lower slopes and valleys around the mountain. The rocks are of value, as miners and prospectors have testified for a century, and the waters that flow from the snow and ice nurture fish and provide hydroelectric power. The region is prime recreation country, a place for fishing, hunting, skiing or simply sitting beneath a great fir tree and contemplating the wonder of it all. As the twentieth century progressed and the press of human needs increased, there grew considerable debate, political and otherwise, about how the resource values of the area should be used and managed.

Very early in the century, as has been noted, some groups believed that Mount Baker region's greatest value lay in its recreational potential. If this potential could be developed, they argued, it would prove a great boon to all of northwestern Washington. Development proceeded, but a great national depression and then a world war intervened, and development failed to yield the fruits that many expected. After the war, the nation's economy began to boom, and demand for lumber for construction increased markedly. Recreation demand increased as well, and the United States Forest Service faced the task of meeting and mediating the diverse demands that people placed on their forest resources. This had never been easy when the population was sparse and demands light; it became ever more difficult as the nation prospered and the population grew.

The Mount Baker region, as earlier described, was made a forest reserve in 1897 and was administered by the Department of the Interior. Then, in 1905, the reserve was transferred to the jurisdiction of the Department of Agriculture. Between 1910 and 1917 there was discussion of a Mount Baker National Park, which would have meant transfer back to the Department of the Interior. The original park plan was scuttled by World War I, but this did not end the argument over who should administer the area and for what purpose. The debate continues, sometimes heating up and reaching public attention and the ears of legislators in Washington, D.C. The history of this debate is an interesting one, important to an understanding of the current situation on and around Mount Baker and its future prospects.

In 1917, prior to the United States entering World War I, hearings were held on the Mount Baker National Park bills introduced in the Sixty-fifth U.S. Congress, and there was much support for them. The Departments of Agriculture and Interior reported to congressional committees: Agriculture was solidly against a park, Interior solidly for it. The war intervened and stalled the initiative, but after the war the bills were reintroduced into the Sixty-sixth Congress. Once again they died in committee. Perhaps the pro-park forces had exhausted their resources and energy in their pre-war promotion; whatever the reason, the park idea went back into incubation. The Forest Service went about the business of extending its supervision and control of the Mount Baker National Forest.

In 1926 the Secretary of Agriculture established the Mount Baker National Park Division of the Forest. This division, which came to be known as the Mount Baker Recreation Area, encompassed 74,859 acres. The designation gave recognition to the exceptional recreational value of the peak and its surrounding ridges and valleys. It was the politic thing to do. The Mount Baker Lodge was soon to open, and everyone was most enthusiastic about the future of recreation at Heather Meadows and elsewhere on and around Mount Baker. The Forest Service had cooperated fully with the Mount Baker Development Company, and everyone seemed to be satisfied with the agency's management of the region. Further, establishment of the recreation area would allow logging, mining and water development projects in the protected division, as long as such projects did not impair its recreational values. Everyone's interests would be served, and the Forest Service hoped that it would not be bothered by further park proposals.

All was quiet for eight years until the Bellingham Chamber of Commerce adopted a resolution in 1934 calling for a park of 74,759 acres, to include both Mount Baker and Mount Shuksan. Once again the intent of the proposal was "toward developing the recreational advantages of the district."[1] Bert Huntoon presented the resolution, which in part pointed out that

> under the laws and regulations governing the administration of national forests, the national forest service has very limited funds and no organization to develop adequate facilities for the convenience, pleasure and comfort of the tourist . . . whereas, the national park service has the funds, organization and facilities to develop and make adequate use of the said area for national recreation purposes and to administer the same.[2]

Progress toward full recreational development had slowed at Heather Meadows and in the Mount Baker area generally, due in large part to the Depression. Undoubtedly the Bellingham Chamber sought a stimulant for its developmental aspirations. Perhaps it thought the resolution might motivate the Forest Service. Ironically, that agency, with the extensive labor of the Civilian Conservation Corps available, was beginning the greatest effort in recreational development that the area was to experience.

Nothing came of the resolution, though interest in national park status for the area was reviving in other quarters. That same year the Land Planning Committee of the National Resources Board proposed national park status for several of the most scenic volcanic peaks in Washington, among them Mount Baker. Three years later the Director of the National Park Service appointed a special committee to investigate the park potential of the Cascades. This committee's report recommended a massive park of some five thousand square miles, which would include all of the major volcanoes in the state of Washington, from Baker in the north to Adams and St. Helens in the south. Their proposal came to be known as "Ice Peaks National Park." It raised a storm of protest. Miners, loggers and diverse others interested in exploiting the resources of the Cascades protested that their business would be severely curtailed, if not eliminated, were such vast acreage devoted to a park. The purpose of a national park is in part, after all, to preserve and protect the beauty and integrity of natural areas, and the proponents of development rightly saw such protection as incompatible with their aspirations. In response to their concerns the National Park Service, the Forest Service and the Washington State Planning Council all launched more studies of the Cascades. Public hearings were held, and in 1940 the National Park Service submitted another report, which called for a Cascades National Park. It would include the glacier-bearing peaks, Mount Baker among them, though it was not on the same grand scale of the 1938 proposal. The Forest Service, not surprisingly, endorsed continuing Forest Service management and opposed any park proposals. The Washington State Planning Council also opposed any parks in the Cascades.

This flurry of proposals and studies revealed a conflict that was to characterize all future discussion of Cascade mountain resource policies. In the cover letter to its "Cascade Mountain Study," the Chairman of the Washington State Planning Council noted the Council's opposition to National Park Service management of the Cascades: "If either plan were adopted, large areas would no doubt be removed from the forest reserves and their wealth of forest and other natural resources would either be completely locked up or their development seriously hampered."[3] From this moment on in the resource management debate it would be the developers versus the preservers. Until the Ice Peaks proposal was unveiled, the proponents of national park status for Mount Baker had themselves been developers, though their interest had been primarily recreational development. They had also been local people. The state's study, however, indicated that people living near the mountains were becoming aware of "abundant natural resources," that they were entering a "phase of discovery and development" and that they wanted minimal interference by the Federal Government in their efforts to develop what they discovered.[4]

World War II reduced interest in new parks, and Mount Baker remained in the National Forest. Twenty years passed, during which the Forest Service managed the Mount Baker region under a multiple-use policy. Some investment was made in recreational development during this time, but it was also a period of increased emphasis on timber production. Roads were extended or built in valleys around the mountain, and clearcuts blossomed along these advancing thoroughfares. Throughout the Cascade Range, extensive road building and logging were the rule, and as the 1950s progressed, concern rose in some quarters that the scenic and recreational values of the mountains were being sacrificed to "commodity production": the extraction of timber, minerals and other resources.

This concern was heard in Washington, D.C., and in 1960 bills were introduced into the Eighty-sixth Congress to provide for studies by the Departments of the Interior and Agriculture of the advisability of establishing a national park in the central and northern Cascades. No congressional action was taken, and similar bills were introduced in the next session. Again there was no congressional action, but the Secretary of Agriculture stopped all logging and roadbuilding in twenty specified areas in the North Cascades until a high-mountain management policy could be written. Support for a national park in the North Cascades continued to grow.

A group of conservationists joined to form the North Cascades Conservation Council. In 1963 they issued a proposal for a 1,038,665-acre North Cascades National Park and a 269,521-acre Chelan National Mountain Recreation Area. Mount Baker was not included in their proposal.[5] That same

Mount Baker from Table Mountain Trail

year a "new era of cooperation" between the traditionally antagonistic Departments of the Interior and Agriculture was announced in a joint letter sent to President Kennedy by their Secretaries. Among its proposals for cooperation was a joint study "of the Federal lands in the North Cascade Mountains of Washington to determine the management and administration of those lands that will best serve the public interest."[6] Soon a study team was appointed to visit the mountains, hold public hearings and issue a report.

Their "North Cascades Study Report," released in 1965, recommended establishment of four new wilderness areas (the Wilderness Act, passed by Congress the preceding September, provided for establishment of a National Wilderness Preservation System), a North Cascades National Park including Mount Shuksan, additions to Mount Rainier National Park and development of an adequate system of scenic roads. One road was recommended to go from Heather Meadows to Baker Lake, through a tunnel under Austin Pass. Mount Baker was excluded from the proposed park. The mountain "and most of the surrounding Recreation Area should continue to be administered by the Forest Service in accord with that agency's plans for development . . ."[7]

The report was intended to suggest legislation that might resolve the long-standing argument between the various groups and agencies vying for use and control of the high Cascades. Its recommendations were a compromise. It included letters to the study team leader from George Selke, a consultant to the Secretary of Agriculture, and George B. Hartzog, Jr., Director of the National Park Service. Selke wrote that he was not pleased with the final recommendations, for he was opposed to the idea of any new national park in the State of Washington.

Certainly, the Mount Baker and Mount Shuksan area has National Park quality. But would it serve the State and Nation better as a National Park than it does now as a full-year outdoor recreation area? . . . My contention is that the extreme northern part of the North Cascades, even Mt. Baker and Mt. Shuksan, have too short a season and too much inclement weather during three-fourths of the year to become a heavily patronized National Park. To become an outstanding recreation area, which it is now and was set aside to be 50 years ago, with year-round active outdoor recreation is still a wiser proposal.[8]

Selke thought that the Forest Service should continue to manage the area. Hartzog was not pleased with the study team's recommendations either, but for entirely different reasons.

> I must . . . object strongly to your deletion of the Nooksack Valley. Especially, do I object strenuously to your deletion of Mount Baker.
>
> . . . Mount Baker affords a splendid area for development of visitor use facilities. More importantly, Mount Baker, with Mount Shuksan and the Pickett Range, is the only sector of the Cascade Range where features illustrating all chapters in the geological story of the Cascade Range from pre-Tertiary times to the present can be presented. Mount Baker and its immediate vicinity are indispensable to the completion of this geologic record. To tear it out . . . as you propose, is to rupture the basis on which the interpretive story of this unique area may be told to its fullest scientific value and in its most dramatic manner.
>
> Your failure to include Mount Baker as we have recommended is even more startling and confusing when one realizes that, as long ago as 1926, the Secretary of Agriculture recognized the national significance and park-like character of Mount Baker by designating it the Mount Baker Park division of the Mount Baker National Forest. Thus, for almost 40 years, by Secretarial Order, the Forest Service has given Mount Baker a special and unique management in recognition of its superlative scenic and scientific values. . . . My principal objection to your deletion of Mount Baker is that, recognizing the park values of Mount Baker, it violates the Congressional missions assigned our respective Services to continue the management of this park area in the Forest Service. . . . to continue the management . . . as suggested in your recommendation, is as incongruous as would be a recommendation that the timber resources of one of the National Forests be assigned to this Service for commercial, sustained yield management.[9]

Despite Hartzog's persuasive arguments, Mount Baker was not to be included in the National Park.

Mount Shuksan in winter, from Picture Lake

On January 30, 1967, President Lyndon Johnson presented a message to the Ninetieth Congress recommending that it establish a national park in the North Cascades. Further work was done on a legislative proposal, and in March a bill was introduced in the United States Senate to establish a North Cascades National Park and Ross Lake National Recreation Area. After much debate and public testimony, a bill was passed in 1968 which created the park and several wilderness and recreation areas. Right to the end, conservationists and the National Park Service urged that the proposed park be enlarged by 135,580 acres in the Mount Baker region, but it was not to be. Mount Shuksan was included, but the boundary was drawn to exclude the scenic Tomyhoi-Selesia area with its metallic mineral deposits (site of Lone Jack and other claims) and the Mount Baker-Baker Lake region with its stands of timber. After nearly sixty years of discussion, the National Park Service took over management of a significant portion of the North Cascades, but not of Mount Baker.

The argument over management of Mount Baker did not end with establishment of the park. During the years since that momentous event there has been almost continuous discussion between various groups about the mountain. Logging has continued, with new roads built and old ones extended. The number of people coming to the area for recreation has increased significantly both in winter and summer. The Mount Baker Ski Area, descendant of the original Mount Baker Development Company's resort, has continued to expand at Heather Meadows, adding new chairlifts and other facilities (one chair in 1960, four in 1970, six by 1980). In summer the meadows are packed with sightseers. Hundreds of hikers and climbers visit the Kulshan Cabin area on a busy weekend. Trails throughout the area are heavily used; the impact on fragile alpine ecosystems is severe in some places.

The paramount issue in managing the area since 1968 has proved to be the mediation of this high demand for recreation and scenic beauty with the demand for timber. This has been translated into the question of how much, if any, of the Mount Baker country should be preserved in its wild state and managed for wilderness recreation. By the 1970s a quarter of a million acres in the area remained wild. It was a *de facto* wilderness. Throughout the United States dozens of National Forest areas were being proposed and studied for addition to the National Wilderness Preservation System, which had been established in 1964. New areas were constantly being identified, and numerous battles raged between developers and preservationists. While no such struggle was occurring over Mount Baker country, the region was affected by other contests when, in 1972, the Forest Service undertook to identify all roadless, undeveloped areas in its jurisdiction that would be good candidates for wilderness classification.

This Roadless Area Review and Evaluation (RARE) involved holding public hearings and studying management alternatives for each roadless area. It attempted to plumb public desires regarding the areas under study and to apply specific criteria to determine whether each area should be studied further for inclusion in the wilderness system or opened to development. The motivation behind RARE was, in large part, to resolve the issue so that "commodity production," as development was euphemistically called in the discussions, could proceed in areas judged unworthy of future consideration as wilderness.

Management alternatives were generated for the 275,000 roadless acres on and around Mount Baker. They ranged from no wilderness to all wilderness. Hearings were held; interested parties waited for announcement of the results. No announcement was made, for the RARE process was inadequate and the results inconclusive. There was pressure to decide rapidly which areas should be considered for wilderness and which "released" to the commodity producers. Criteria for inventory were too general and some roadless areas were missed in the process. The Forest Service would not make specific recommendations for fear of litigation, so it decided further inventory was necessary, building on the work done in RARE.

The next review process, which began in June 1977, was called RARE II. It identified 2,919 roadless areas in national forests nationwide, including the Mount Baker region. After considering various factors, including public comment, existing laws and regulations, identified public needs and the professional judgment of Department of Agriculture personnel, the Forest Service made its recommendations to the Secretary of Agriculture. Of the three alternatives that could be recommended for each area—wilderness, nonwilderness or future study—Mount Baker was declared nonwilderness.

One study after another testified to the unique nature of Mount Baker and its surroundings. Yet once again long-term protection of its wild and scenic beauty was denied, even though the area was rated high for its wilderness "attributes." Unfortunately for wilderness advocates, the area also contains valuable timber and minerals.[10] It seems likely that the decision to recommend nonwilderness status for the Mount Baker study area, as indeed for most study areas in Washington, came from the belief that there were already sufficient lands protected as park and wilderness in the state. A value judgment based on the data collected, agency desires and politics elevated commercial forestry over "dispersed recreation" and the unquantifiable values of wild and beautiful country. As the record shows, the Forest Service has struggled for seventy-five years to keep itself unfettered in its management of the Mount Baker area; throughout that time emphasis on timber harvesting has been increasing. The RARE II decision was another episode in the long history of Forest Service opposition to what it has perceived as an effort to restrict the options for management of the Mount Baker country.

The studies may be complete, at least for a time, but the argument goes on. When the wilderness inventories failed to offer the remaining Mount Baker wilderness any protection from the saw and bulldozer, a group of spiritual descendants of Mount Baker enthusiasts formed the Mount Baker Wilderness Association. They hoped to use the procedures of the Wilderness Act of 1964 to gain protection for an area that they believed met the criteria for wilderness, despite what the Forest Service might have to say about it. Aware of the service's long-standing opposition to any but multiple-use management of the area, these people were not surprised at the RARE II recommendation.

The Wilderness Act of 1964 defined wilderness as follows:

> A wilderness . . . is hereby recognized as an area where the earth and its community of life are untrammeled by man, where man himself is a visitor who does not remain . . . is . . . an area of undeveloped Federal land retaining its primeval character and influence, without permanent improvements or human habitation, which is protected and managed so as to preserve its natural conditions . . . .[11]

The Association has identified approximately 235,000 acres which it feels meet the criteria specified in the Act. The centerpiece of the proposed area is, of course, Mount Baker. The wilderness area is divided into four major sections:

North Section: Here exist the even topped ridges which run along the U.S.-Canadian border. Several large peaks and buttes are present, the highest being over 8,000 feet. Numerous alpine lakes are included along with the larger Tomyhoi Lake which is over 4,000 feet below the walls of surrounding peaks. Several virgin valleys are located within the section.

Central Section: This area is dominated by the massive rock and ice formations of Mount Baker. Surrounding ridges provide awesome vistas of active glaciation. The southwest side of the mountain gives way to large open meadows which descend to Swift Creek near Baker Lake.

West Section: This area displays the unique geological formation of the Twin Sisters peaks as well as providing the vital headwaters of the Nooksack River. Erosion of this comparatively soft material has produced strikingly beautiful formations.

South Section: Consists of rolling high country east and south of Baker Lake. Between sparsely wooded highlands and heavily forested valleys, this area provides an excellent example of environmental stratas and has great value as one of the few complete subalpine systems on the western slope of the Cascades.[12]

Mount Baker from the northeast

All of the area is de facto wilderness, country which has escaped the incursions of humans because it was hard to get to and commodities could be more easily extracted elsewhere. There are no roads into it. Hikers, climbers and fishermen use it extensively. The RARE II recommendation may open the entire forested area for timber harvest and other commodity production. Association members note that the study identified 107,600 acres of the 275,000 roadless acres inventoried as commercial forestland. This includes 17,000 would-be commercial acres in the Mount Baker Recreation Area. Since 1926 these acres have been exempted from allowable-cut calculations. Thus the group feels that some of the most scenic land, long valued for recreation, will be yielded to loggers.

The Forest Service argues that there is nothing to fear; that it will continue to consider the interests of those who love scenery and wild country; that it will concern itself with the welfare of the rare plant and animal species within the area. The agency claims it has done so for almost eighty years, why should it cease to do so now? The answer to that question, wilderness proponents argue, lies in Washington, D.C., where bureaucrats and politicians—eyes fixed only on the financial balance sheet, economic indicators and budgets, their ears full of the persuasions of timber industry lobbyists—consider the future of the nation's resources. Leaving the disposition to them, preservationists suggest, is leaving too much to people unfamiliar with the values at stake. Since RARE II there has been a push to quickly release all land designated for nonwilderness for commodity production.

Recent events in California have made it unlikely that any conclusion regarding land use on Mount Baker will come from RARE II. The Ninth Circuit Court of Appeals ruled in January of 1983 that the RARE II Environmental Impact Statement was legally insufficient in evaluating California's roadless areas for wilderness. The court ruled that development in wilderness could not proceed until studies were made of specific effects on the sites in question. This ruling blocked the intended outcome of the RARE II process.

While the Forest Service was deciding how to respond to this ruling, Washington Senators Henry Jackson and Slade Gorton introduced the Washington State Wilderness Act of 1983 in Congress. Their bill had two parts, one presenting the RARE II wilderness recommendations for Washington State, the other identifying areas excluded from RARE II wilderness recommendations that would be debated in Congress for possible reclassification as wilderness areas. One such area was Mount Baker. The Jackson-Gorton bill made no specific recommendations regarding boundaries and acreage, but it reopened the possibility that at least some of the de facto wilderness around Mount Baker might be preserved as part of the National Wilderness Preservation System.

Other legislation concerning Washington wilderness has been introduced in Congress; it is likely that a resolution of the wilderness question may come in 1984. All sides favor a decision. How much wilderness will be preserved is uncertain, but it is possible that some part of the Mount Baker region will become a legally protected wilderness area. Perhaps, seventy-eight years after the idea of preserving the beauties of the region first occurred to someone, action will be taken.

So, the argument rages on. It will continue until the wilderness is gone or is protected. This episode in the Mount Baker story is one of studies and reports, congressional bills and thousands of pages of argument. Dry stuff it is, far removed from the excitement and romance of prospecting, mountaineering and marathon racing, but it is important. Time after time the Mount Baker country has been proposed for park and wilderness status, and time after time the decision has been made for multiple use. The Mount Baker story so far is one of adventure on a wild, beautiful and rugged landscape. It is a story of risk and uncertainty, of prospectors, mountaineers, even busi-

nessmen launching ventures where the successful outcome of their endeav-
ors was far from assured, where the powers of nature, unfettered by human
technology, might repel or even crush them. Are the days gone when such
risk and adventure can be taken here? Not yet, but the outcome of the arguments between those who would preserve scenic beauty and wildness and
those who would reduce or destroy it will determine whether there will be
much more such adventuring on and around the mountain.

The urban mountaineers from Portland's Mazamas who sat around
their campfire at Mazama Park in 1909 would surely be amazed at the seventy years of argument that followed their introduction of the Mount Baker
National Park idea. They could not envision the changes that have come
and would be chagrined to learn that "their" mountain remains unprotected
today. There may or may not be a park or wilderness area in its future, but
surely there will be people like those early Mazamas who will wish, argue
and agitate for one. The decades of debate over management of Mount
Baker has established one point beyond doubt. It is, in George Selke's
words, an "outstanding recreation area" of "National Park quality." This
quality will not change unless its human caretakers mismanage it.

13

Present and Future

The world is circumscribed. The surface of this little earth of ours is limited, and we cannot add to it. . . . All we can do is to turn it to the best possible account. Now, let us remember that the quantity of natural beauty in the world, the number of spots calculated to give enjoyment in the highest form, are limited, and are being constantly encroached upon.
—James Bryce, 1913

Mount Baker and the country surrounding it cannot and will not remain unchanged. Human effort and natural processes will work inexorable transformation upon the landscape. This has been true over the relatively short span of time chronicled here, and while it is impossible to predict whether change in the near future will be as dramatic as in the recent past, it is likely that it will. Our demand for resources is increasing very rapidly, and there are resources on and around the mountain that are being exploited and considered for development.

Development has proceeded throughout the region. The Mount Baker Ski Area, in particular, has flourished. It reopened after World War II but had some rough years. By the early 1950s the Korean War was draining resources, and use of the area was reduced so much that the state highway department considered closing the road once more during the winter. Local businessmen came to the rescue: they bought out the struggling Mount Baker Lodge Company and formed a new one, the Mount Baker Recreation Company. Better capitalized and managed than its predecessor, it was able to install the chairlift equipment necessary to attract skiers. By 1957 the operation began to make money. Its

Mount Baker ski lift

major market proved to be Canadians from Vancouver, British Columbia.

Skiing grew rapidly in the late 1950s and early 1960s. Trying to keep up with demand, indeed to increase it, the new company installed many facilities and rope tows. By mid 1965 a second chairlift went into operation; a fourth and fifth were installed in 1968 and 1969. Area lifts could carry some five thousand skiers up the slopes each hour, and new lifts continued to open new terrain for skiers of all abilities. A sewage treatment plant and a day lodge were operating in 1971. Two more chairlifts were built in 1974 and 1978, and despite several poor snow years, the company continued to make a profit. There is often snow on the slopes of the Mount Baker Ski Area when it is too sparse for skiing anywhere else in the Northwest, so the area is known for its early- and late-season skiing. On a good day at the peak of the season, as many as four thousand skiers are on the slopes. The ski business has progressed a long way since a few hardy enthusiasts struggled up to Heather Meadows in the late 1920s, when the lodge lay quiet under many feet of snow, and they had all they could do to get in a couple of runs a day.

The ski area, however, has no monopoly of skiing in the vicinity of Mount Baker. In recent years there has been a dramatic increase in cross-country skiers, of whom Happy Fisher, Ben Thompson and the other pioneers of skiing in the Mount Baker region would doubtless approve. These skiers have no need for the Recreation Company's facilities. They fasten on their "skinny skis" and set out along low country roads or onto the open slopes around the ski area. On the south side of Mount Baker they compete with snowmobiles in the Schrieber's Meadows area. Skiers and snow-mobilers alike climb high onto the south slopes of the mountain itself on good winter days. Near the ski area ski-touring parties travel around Table Mountain or to Herman Saddle and Artist Point. When avalanche conditions permit, they make superb runs off the northern face of Table Mountain or down the open slopes of Mount Herman. Spurning crowds and lifts, they may climb upward for an entire day to make one long run through unbroken powder. Equipment and technique recently have been changing and improving; this approach to skiing may continue to draw an increasing number in the future.

In recent years helicopters have been seen occasionally on good winter days, coming and going from the ski area with alpine skiers (as opposed to nordic skiers) to good powder skiing in the nearby mountains. The prevalent bad weather and great amounts of snowfall in a normal winter, with consequent avalanche hazard, limits this approach to skiing. It is expensive as well, but there may be more of it in the future. Of course, people also climb Mount Baker in spring and summer for glacier skiing. This has its risks, but there will always be adventurers willing to take them for the rewards of year-round skiing and extreme tests of skill. In all, it seems safe to predict that skiing will continue to be popular around Mount Baker.

The timber industry has also been at work during this period, extending logging roads, building new ones and lobbying at all levels to get their crews into more and more old-growth timber in the Mount Baker National Forest. The thirty-year period prior to 1980 was one of relative prosperity in America. The settlement patterns of the nation reflected this, as city dwellers moved to the surrounding country and built dream homes in the suburbs. Demand for lumber increased throughout the period, and old-growth forests on private land were cut down quickly. As private timber stocks were depleted, the pressure on the National Forests to harvest their timber has mounted.

In 1950 the upper valley of the Middle Fork of the Nooksack River was almost as wild as it had been in the days of Edmund Coleman. The Deming Trail was a popular recreation route into the scenic region south of Mount Baker, but the valley had not been changed by the logger's saw. Pressure to log the valley increased until, in 1962, a great windstorm struck the Pacific Northwest and blew down many old trees. The forests of the Middle Fork did not escape, though damage there was not as severe as in many other areas. Still, the timber industry and those in the Forest Service who had long wished to log in the valley argued that they must go in and harvest the blow-downs before they were wasted; thus came logging to the upper Middle Fork. A road was built up the valley in the mid-1960s, and logging has been extensive ever since. Logging roads reach high up the ridges on both sides of the river, and up tributary streams. Clearcuts gape high on Marmot and Grouse Ridges immediately west of the main uplift of Mount Baker.

Logging roads had also moved into virgin timber and up toward timberline further to the east in the Baker River Ranger District. In a major developmental thrust, a private utility company built a hydroelectric dam on the upper Baker River, and in 1959 the five-thousand-acre basin behind the dam was filling, covering old Baker Lake. As part of this development initiative, roads for logging and recreation were constructed, one reaching six miles up Swift Creek to Baker Hot Springs, another 10 miles up to Shuksan Creek and a third nine miles up Sulphur Creek to Schrieber's Meadows not far from timberline on Baker's southern side. These roads significantly increased use of this scenic area. There was consideration of extending Shuksan Creek Road to meet Mount Baker Highway at Austin Pass (presumably through the tunnel under Austin Pass), but nothing has come of that idea.

The greatest period of mining and prospecting activity, around the turn of the century, provided the impetus for development of roads and other improvements up the North Fork of the Nooksack River. There was also considerable prospecting and some effort at mining by Joe Morovits and others on the Baker Lake side of the mountain. Mining operations in the region, except at the Lone Jack and Boundary Red mines near the Canadian border, were never very profitable. Gold was produced at Lone Jack until 1924, at Boundary Red until 1942. There were, however, more than five thousand mining claims staked in the Mount Baker Mining District from 1890 to 1937.[1] From time to time, there have been attempts to work some of these claims, but none have produced any significant returns on effort and investment. The prices of metallic minerals have not been high enough to merit much exploitation of deposits in the area. There was hope, for instance, in 1950 that some of the claims in the Twin Lakes area would once again be worth working. The Twin Lakes Road was extended 4.8 miles above Shuksan to the lakes, but by the time it was complete mineral values were going down and prospectors had left the area. No development beyond the road construction was accomplished.

Some nonmetallic minerals also have been mined. The Glacier Coalfield, six miles northwest of Mount Baker, was discovered early in the century, west and upslope from Glacier Creek. Containing both anthracite and bituminous coal, it has been mined from time to time and is currently worked on a small scale. On Wells Creek there has also been quarrying of andesite for building stone. The Twin Sisters range, composed entirely of olivine, constitutes one of the largest available concentrations of this mineral in North America. In 1963 quarrying operations were begun in the northwestern end of Twin Sisters Mountain at an elevation of about 2,600 feet. The olivine was processed for foundary sand.

Interest in mineral deposits in the region has continued. When the price of gold shot up late in the 1970s, prospectors went back into the hills. Then the price went down again; no major mining operations were begun. But the mineral deposits are still there and may one day be valuable, so exploration for them continues. The presence of minerals in the area was given as one of several reasons why the Mount Baker country should not be made into a park or wilderness area. Undoubtedly mineral values will continue to fluctuate as American and world industry and technology change. It seems likely that there will be mining of one mineral or another in the region's future.

The fire lookouts have been replaced by aircraft surveillance. Most lookout houses are gone, though Winchester Mountain to the north of Mount Baker and Park Butte to the South still hold theirs. Park Butte Lookout has been maintained for some years by the Skagit Alpine Club. The cabin on Winchester Mountain was recently adopted by the Mount Baker Hiking Club, direct descendant of the Mount Baker Club. The club has also adopted the trail from Twin Lakes to the lookout. These groups maintain the lookouts to preserve a bit of history and a destination for club outings. Increasingly the Forest Service is encouraging outdoor organizations to offset reduced funding for recreation by volunteering their time and resources to maintain the area's recreational and cultural resources.

There has been discussion in recent years about Kulshan Cabin, which is the property of the students of Western Washington University. For thirty years the cabin was a popular destination for college outings, and the university shared responsibility for it with the Mount Baker Club. Then, total responsibility for it devolved to the University. Though the cabin is no longer used extensively for university-sponsored activities, it is the summer destination for thousands of day hikers and climbers from all over the Northwest, even all of North America. As a result, the area has suffered from the heavy use and occasional misuse by people who contribute nothing to its maintenance. For a decade students have stationed a caretaker at the cabin to maintain and protect it during periods of peak summer usage. But money is tight in the 1980s, and the University has serious reservations about continuing its involvement with the building. The Forest Service cannot maintain it, so this historic timberline attraction may vanish, like almost all of the other cabins and lookouts in Mount Baker country.

What can be said about the future of the Mount Baker region? As noted earlier, the arguments over its management will continue as long as there are some people who want to harvest trees and others who want to preserve them. The Forest Service will continue to struggle with the conflicting demands of various interest groups. It recognizes that demand for both timber and "primitive recreation" will increase. The Draft Pacific Northwest Region Plan notes the problem:

> The Region does not have the capability to meet projected demand for wilderness-type use within the wilderness system. Wilderness use will increase not only as a function of population but also as use in presently undeveloped areas is displaced by other resource activities. By approximately the year 1985, the Region will not have the capability to meet the demand for this type of recreation within the wilderness system.[2]

The demand for timber from the National Forests will also rise, as reported in a Congressional Budget Office study.

> Several studies have concluded that (in the Pacific Northwest) the stock of second-growth timber will be too small to replace the decline of old-growth inventories and maintain production levels from private lands through the next 5 to 20 years. Consequently, allocation of a larger portion of the present inventory of National Forest old growth to sales during the 1980s would greatly increase the possibility of regional shortages in 10 to 30 years, if the increase in National Forest sales cannot be sustained.[3]

Indeed, there is increasing pressure to cut National Forest timber in the Northwest. The Forest Service has tried for years to regulate the harvest closely on a "nondeclining even flow" basis that will allow a steady level of timber supply for the future.[4] In 1984 there are strong pressures to abandon this management policy and to cut, at least for a while, at a rate that cannot be sustained. This bodes ill both for the future of the timber industry in the Mount Baker region and for recreation. These two pressures—greater demand for recreation and greater demand for timber production—will clash in the Northwest, and Mount Baker's forests will be the source of contention. At present support for greater timber production seems to have the upper hand.

Development in the near future will take new forms. Seattle City Light, the public utility that provides electricity for Seattle, is patiently working its way through procedures that will allow it to explore the geothermal energy potential of some 93,000 acres around Mount Baker. Drilling rigs will undoubtedly work the area south of the mountain in the vicinity of Schrieber's Meadows, Baker Hot Springs and Swift Creek in hopes that geothermal fields will be revealed. If they find fields of sufficient potential, installations will be built to convert the heat to electricity, and transmission lines will carry it to the main transmission system. It is impossible to say right now whether much geothermal development in the area is likely (some experts are skeptical), but if such development occurs, another corner of the Mount Baker region will be transformed.

Geothermal is not the only energy potential under investigation. There is also much interest in small hydroelectric development. Small streams with steep gradients can turn small generators to contribute to electricity production. Each stream will not produce a great amount of electrical energy alone, but if many streams are harnessed they could add up to a significant contribution. In 1984, for instance, two companies are proceeding with plans to develop small hydro projects on four streams (Sulphur, Rocky, Sandy and Dillard Creeks) on Baker's south side. Dozens of other potential small hydro sites have been identified in the region. There are many problems to be surmounted before construction work begins on such projects, but with power demands increasing and alternative sources of power held up by various technical, economic and environmental difficulties, "clean" sources of energy like geothermal and small hydro are likely to be pursued.

A geothermal plant or a few small hydro operations might not affect the mountain country very much. But if such projects become concentrated in one area, such as the southern slopes of Mount Baker, then the change in the landscape might be considerable. The Forest Service intends to impose some limitations on development. For example, the draft environmental assessment for geothermal leasing prohibits geothermal exploration in areas where it would interfere with recreation. Exploration will not be allowed in the Heather Meadows area, nor along streams and lakeshores. The document affirms that exploration must go forward because it is consistent with national goals, policy and direction, but that it will be done in the least environmentally disruptive manner possible. Time will tell what changes all of this will bring to Mount Baker, but it seems certain that human enterprise will continue to encroach upon the mountain unless it is stopped by some policy of preservation.

One potential change has nothing to do with human enterprise, the force of volcanism. No one can predict that Mount Baker will become volcanically active at any specific time in the future, but most experts believe that future activity is likely. It is a young volcano, in geologic terms. And as Mount St. Helens recently demonstrated, such a volcano might violently spring to life at any time without warning.

Mount Baker's activity could take several forms, with various consequences for the surrounding country. Geologists have found evidence of several types of activity: toxic gas emissions, lava flows, earthquakes, mudflows, rock avalanches and pyroclastic flows (a mass of hot, dry rock debris moving viscously downslope under the influence of gravity).[5] Any of these events, along with associated floods, could occur in one eruptive episode. It might begin with increased thermal activity, which occurs constantly at a low level in Sherman Crater and the Dorr Fumaroles. Geologists would respond by installing monitoring equipment on the mountain to measure gas composition, heat, tilt of slopes and seismic activity. If it began to warm up or if earthquakes within the mountain were detected, measures would be taken to warn people in areas that might be affected by an eruption, such as those living on the floodplains of the Skagit and Nooksack rivers. People in Glacier, Kulshan and near Baker Lake would perhaps be evacuated. The mountain would be closed to climbing and hiking.

The most likely geologic hazard concerning officials would be the possibility of mudflows or rock avalanches. A rock debris avalanche, such as might come off Sherman Peak, could trigger a mudflow. The worst case would be for such a mudflow to roar down Boulder Glacier into Baker Lake, or down the southern side into the Middle Fork valley. Similar slides might come off the western and northern sides of the mountain, moving down Glacier Creek. The impact would depend, of course, on the flow's size, but a large mudflow could well flood the town of Glacier or bury it in mud. A large mudflow into Baker Lake could send a flood surging down the Baker and Skagit rivers, perhaps damaging Baker River dams, releasing impounded water and creating even greater floods in the lowlands.

In 1975 the increased thermal activity in Sherman Crater caused a lake to be impounded. Geologists feared that the heating might weaken already unstable mud and rock in the crater, result in a slide and send mud and water down the slope. This did not occur, but it could happen in the future. Floods might also occur if pyroclastic or lava flows spilled onto Baker's large glaciers and snowfields. Evidence of one pyroclastic flow has been found to have occurred 8,700 years ago. While unlikely, such a flow could occur again. Lava flows have been more common; their principal hazards are melting and flooding.

It is difficult to imagine the effects of a major, explosive eruption of Mount Baker. Mount St. Helens was quite dramatic, but there is no reason to believe anything on a similar scale is likely to occur on Mount Baker. Still, the possibility is there, and people living in areas of potential hazard have to consider it. Emergency services agencies must think about their response to a volcanic emergency but hope that science has learned enough to be able to predict any upcoming cataclysms. Perhaps such forecasts will be routine by the time Mount Baker stirs, but its current population should always respect the sleeping giant, even as the Indians living around it did in the past.

The future of the area will, then, barring a great natural or human catastrophe (a vast forest fire, a nuclear war), probably be like the recent past. The "multiple uses" championed by the Forest Service will continue around

Climbers labor up the icy ridge to the Mount Baker summit, just over the dome at top left.

the mountain. Mining, recreation, energy development and logging will most likely increase. Though people will continue to fight to preserve the remaining old-growth forests and wilderness, some will fall to the logger's saw. Primitive recreation opportunities will gradually decrease. Scenery will be spectacular, but trails and meadows will be crowded on good days by sightseers from growing urban areas to the west, particularly the growing Vancouver, British Columbia, metropolitan area.

Increasing pressure on decreasing recreational resources will pose problems for Federal managers. Decisions will have to be made about heavily used areas like those around Table Mountain, near Kulshan Cabin and around Twin Lakes. Undoubtedly some of the freedoms city dwellers seek in the mountains will have to be curtailed. Summer staff will be stationed in heavily used areas to discourage behavior detrimental to the environment and to other people's recreational experience. The North Cascades National Park already applies a very strict user limitation, which adds to the pressure on the National Forest.

As this is written the Forest Service presence in the area is being reduced. The Glacier Ranger Station has been closed, its staff combined with that of the Baker River District and relocated in Sedro Woolley. At the same time, the Forest Service priority has moved away from recreation in recent years. Funds for recreation staff have been reduced, as have those for maintenance of trails and recreational facilities. Recreation is at a low ebb in the agency's priorities. The Forest Service preaches multiple use, but not necessarily equality of uses. Timber production now takes precedence over recreation. If this condition continues, there will be serious erosion of the recreational resource, especially if projections of increased recreational demand are correct.

Climbers will continue to come to Mount Baker. It will be an "experience climb" for each new generation of Northwest mountaineers. The average climber will want to "bag" it sometime in his or her career. Pioneers in the sport have long since moved on to challenges in the British Columbia Coast Range, the Alaska Range or other great ranges, but they will still come to Mount Baker for fun and experience. The "groove" will be worn each year from the hogsback above Kulshan Cabin (or the site of the former cabin, should it be torn down) up Coleman Glacier to the summit. The recent increase in the number of guided parties may continue. Sanitation facilities will have to be installed where climbing parties camp before starting up the Coleman Glacier route—pollution is already a problem every summer. Mountain rescue will be busy as urban-based adventurers, misjudging the scale of a "hike" up the mountain, get into trouble.

This is not a particularly pleasant scenario, especially to people who love the wild beauty of the Mount Baker country, but recent trends and population growth point toward such a future. Perhaps recreation will once again rise to its rightful place among the multiple uses. Perhaps a major jobs program like the Civilian Conservation Corps will contribute the people and resources necessary to work on conservation problems. Perhaps preservationists will prevail and a Mount Baker wilderness or park of some size will be established. Any or all of these events could alter the scenario, but whatever happens, the story of Mount Baker will be one of change, as interesting as it has been up to the present.

Notes

Chapter 1

1. Many details of Coleman's attempts on Mount Baker are from his article "Mountaineering on the Pacific," *Harpers New Monthly Magazine* 39(November 1869): 793-817. The entire article with annotations is in Harry M. Majors, ed., *Mount Baker: A Chronicle of Its Historic Eruptions and First Ascent* (Seattle: Northwest Press, 1978).
2. Harry M. Majors, ed., *Mount Baker: A Chronicle of Its Historic Eruptions and First Ascent* (Seattle: Northwest Press, 1978), p. 68.
3. Stratton, "Ascent of Mount Baker," *The Weekly Message* (Port Townsend), September 3, 1868, p. 2, and September 10, 1868, p. 1.
4. Ibid.
5. Ibid.
6. Ibid.
7. Majors, *Mount Baker*, pp. 202-7, describes what is known of Coleman's post-Mount Baker career.

Chapter 2

1. June McCormick Collins, *Valley of the Spirits: The Upper Skagit Indians of Western Washington* (Seattle: University of Washington Press, 1974), pp. 21-2.
2. Footnote by Charles M. Buchanan in Theodore Winthrop, *The Canoe and the Saddle* (Tacoma: Williams, 1913), p. 279. Quoted in Majors, *Mount Baker*, p. 16.
3. Brent Calloway and Allan Richardson, "Nooksack Place Names: An Ethnohistorical and Linguistic Approach," *Working Papers for the 18th International Conference on Salish and Neighboring Languages* (Seattle: University of Washington Press, August 1983).
4. Collins, *Valley of the Spirits*, p. 157.
5. Charles M. Buchanan, "The Origin of Mounts Baker and Rainier: The Indian Legend," *The Mountaineer*, 9(December 1916): 32-5.
6. Ella F. Clark, *Indian Legends of the Pacific Northwest* (Berkeley: University of California Press, 1953), p. 8.
7. Ibid.
8. Ibid., p. 43.
9. Charles Finley Easton, "Mount Baker—Its Trails and Legends: Original Discovery of the Entrance to Puget Sound and First View of Mount Baker," *Northwest Journal of Education*, 25, 4.
10. Robert Ballard Whitebrook, *Coastal Exploration of Washington* (Palo Alto: Pacific Books, 1959), pp. 54-63.

11. Majors, *Mount Baker*, p. 12.
12. George Vancouver et. al., *A Voyage of Discovery to the North Pacific Ocean* (London, 1798), vol. 1, pp. 221-22.
13. Collins, *Valley of the Spirits*, p. 32.
14. F.W. Howay, W.N. Sage and H.F. Angus, *British Columbia and the United States* (Toronto: The Ryerson Press, 1942) p. 142.
15. Ibid.

Chapter 3
1. Robert Emmett Hawley, *Skquee Mus: Pioneer Days on the Nooksack* (Bellingham: Whatcom Museum of History and Art, 1971), p. xxi.
2. Easton, "Mount Baker: Its Trails and Legends," Whatcom Museum of History and Art, Bellingham (Unpublished Scrapbook, compiled 1903-1930), p. 42.
3. Ibid.
4. Ibid.
5. Tillicum (pseudonym for L.L. Bales), "A Trip to Mount Baker," *Pacific Magazine* 2(March 1890): 8-9.
6. Ibid.
7. Majors, *Mount Baker*, pp. 208-9.
8. "Ascent of Mount Baker," *The West Shore* (Portland), 10(August 1884): 237.
9. Ibid.
10. Frank Carleton Teck, "Mountain Climbers Who Have Ascended Mount Baker," *Seattle Post-Intelligencer*, July 29, 1906.
11. Easton, p. 43.
12. For the full story of the North Cascades Highway, see JoAnn Roe, *The North Cascadians* (Seattle: Madrona Publishers, 1980).
13. Percival R. Jeffcott, *Cheechaco and Sourdough* (Bellingham: Pioneer Printing Company, 1963), p. 20.

Chapter 4
1. *Whatcom Reveille*, July 8, 1891.
2. Aubrey L. Haines, *Mountain Fever* (Portland: Oregon Historical Society, 1962), p. 225 (footnote).
3. Easton, p. 48.
4. Ibid.
5. Ibid.
6. Ibid., p. 50.
7. A fine work on Hegg is Murray Morgan, *One Man's Gold Rush* (Seattle: University of Washington Press, 1967).
8. *Seattle Post-Intelligencer*, September 19, 1981.
9. Easton, p. 54.
10. Ibid.
11. Ibid.
12. Ibid.
13. Ibid.
14. See Dolly Connelly, "Morovits: The Hospitable Hermit of Baker Lake," *Off Belay*, 26(August 1976): pp. 6-10.
15. A.J. Craven, "Joe Morovits: The Hermit of Mount Baker," in Easton, p. 214.

Chapter 5

1. Easton, p. 57.
2. Accounts of the Heliograph expedition are from Frank Branch Riley, "Struggle with Mount Baker," *Mazama* (1948), p. 51, and M.W. Gorman's letter to Easton, in Easton, p. 59.
3. Ibid., p. 52.
4. Jeffcott, *Cheechaco and Sourdough*, p. 76.
5. Ibid., pp. 83-4.
6. Ibid., p. 83.
7. *Whatcom Reveille*, September 22, 1897.
8. Mary DeBorde, "Glacier: A History" (Glacier, Washington: Mount Baker-Snoqualmie National Forest, 1981), p. 73 (mimeographed).
9. Ibid.
10. Harold C. Criswell, "Historical Sketch—Mount Baker National Forest," *The Mountaineer*, 57, 4(March 1964): 48-49.
11. Ibid., p. 53.
12. C.E. Rusk, *Tales of a Western Mountaineer* (Boston: Houghton Mifflin Company, 1924), pp. 117-35.

Chapter 6

1. John D. Scott, *We Climb High* (Portland: The Mazamas, 1969), p. 13.
2. Ibid.
3. Ibid.
4. Asahel Curtis, "The First Ascent of Mount Shuksan," from *Overland Monthly* (August, 1907), in Easton, p. 70.
5. Ibid.
6. Ibid.
7. R.L. Glisan, "A Night on the Summit of Mount Baker," in Easton, p. 88.
8. Ibid.
9. "With the Mountaineers on Mount Baker," *The Mountaineer*, 1, 4(1908): 88-96.
10. Easton, "Storm Bound on Mt. Baker," *Forest and Stream*, LXXII, 1(January 2, 1909): p. 10.
11. Gertrude Metcalfe Sholes, "The Mount Baker Outing of the Mazamas in 1909," *Mazama*, VI, 1(December 1920): p. 28.
12. Ibid.
13. Ibid., p. 30.

Chapter 7

1. *American-Reveille* (Bellingham), July 11, 1912, editorial.
2. Ibid., August 11, 1911, p. 2.
3. Ibid., July 13, 1912, editorial.
4. Ibid., July 7, 1912, p. 7.
5. Ibid., July 25, 1912, p. 3.
6. Ibid., August 2, 1912.

Chapter 8

1. Scott, *We Climb High*, p. 13.

2. Easton, p. 193.
3. From "official correspondence," quoted by Easton, p. 194.
4. Ibid.
5. Ibid., p. 196.
6. Ibid.
7. Ibid.
8. Ibid., p. 205.
9. For a more detailed description of the Mount Baker Lodge, see Ramon Heller, *Mount Baker Ski Area: A Pictorial History* (Bellingham: Mount Baker Recreation Company, 1980).
10. Fred H. McNeil, "Backtracking Old Trails," *Mazama*, XII, 12(December 1930): 9.
11. L.R. Frazeur, "With the Mountaineers in 1916," *The Mountaineer*, 9(December 1916): 13.
12. Jamieson Parker, "The Mount Baker Outing of 1920," *Mazama*, VI, 1(December 1920): 3-15.
13. Easton, p. 214.
14. Connelly, "Morovits," p. 10.
15. *Bellingham Herald*, July 11, 1960.

Chapter 9
1. See Heller, *Mount Baker Ski Area*, pp. 29-46.
2. DeBorde, "Glacier," pp. 78-82.
3. DeBorde, "Glacier," pp. 71-72.
4. H.H. Long, "Mount Baker Forest Created in 1897, Embraces 1,851,397 Acres," *Bellingham Herald*, June 23, 1940.

Chapter 10
1. Fred Beckey, *Challenge of the North Cascades* (Seattle: The Mountaineers, 1969), pp. 199-200.
2. Ed Cooper, "Climbing Notes," *The Mountaineer*, 1958, pp. 101-2.
3. Fred Beckey, "Climbs and Expeditions," *American Alpine Club Journal*, 1959, p. 305.
4. Ed Cooper, "Climbing Notes," *The Mountaineer*, 1961, p. 100.
5. Ibid.
6. Klindt Vielbig, "Climbing Notes," *The Mountaineer*, 1961, pp. 99-100.
7. Ibid.
8. Cooper, "Climbs and Expeditions—Mount Baker," *American Alpine Club Journal*, 1959, p. 302.
9. Herb Staley, "Climbs and Expeditions—Mount Baker, Lincoln Peak," *American Alpine Club Journal*, 1957, p. 146.
10. Ibid., p. 147.
11. Ibid.
12. Ibid., p. 148.
13. Herb Staley, "Climbing Notes," *The Mountaineer*, 1956, p. 121.
14. Ibid.

Chapter 11

1. William N. Parke, "Report on the 1937 Mount Baker Avalanche Rescue Work" (Washington: Government Printing Office, 1939), p. 4.

Chapter 12

1. Bert Huntoon, speech to Bellingham Chamber of Commerce, in *Mount Baker Scrapbook—1930s,* Mount Baker Hiking Club, Bellingham, Washington.
2. Ibid.
3. B.H. Kiser, "Letter," in *Cascade Mountain Study* (Olympia: Washington State Planning Council, May, 1940).
4. Huntoon, op. cit.
5. J. Michael McCloskey, ed., *Prospectus for a North Cascades National Park* (Seattle: North Cascades Conservation Council, 1963).
6. Orville Freeman and Stewart Udall, "Letter of January 28, 1963, from Secretary of the Interior and Secretary of Agriculture to President Kennedy," in North Cascades Study Team, *The North Cascades* (Washington, D.C.: U.S. Department of the Interior—U.S. Department of Agriculture, October, 1965), pp. 153-4.
7. Ibid., p. 16.
8. Ibid., pp. 134-5.
9. Ibid., p. 140.
10. U.S. Department of Agriculture, Forest Service, "Washington Supplement to Draft Environmental Statement, Roadless Area Review and Evaluation" (Portland: Pacific Northwest Region, Forest Service, June 15, 1978), p. 73.
11. Public Law 88-577, Eighty-eighth Congress, S. 4 (September 3, 1964).
12. Mount Baker Wilderness Association, "Proposed Mt. Baker Wilderness Description" (Bellingham: 1980, unpublished).

Chapter 13

1. Wayne S. Moen, *Mines and Mineral Deposits of Whatcom County, Washington* (Olympia: State of Washington, Department of Natural Resources, 1969), p. 63.
2. United States Department of Agriculture, Forest Service, "Draft: Pacific Northwest Region Plan (Portland: Pacific Northwest Region, Forest Service, July, 1981), p. 36.
3. Congressional Budget Office, "Forest Service Timber Sales: Their Effect on Wood Product Prices," May, 1980.
4. Rice Odell, "National Forest Disputants: At Loggerheads Again," Conservation Foundation Letter (July 1981), p. 5.
5. Kirk A. Johnson, "Mount Baker Risk Analysis: The Effects of a Future Eruption of Mount Baker to the People and Property of Whatcom County, Washington" (Bellingham: Western Washington University, Department of Geology, 1981, unpublished).

Bibliography

Natural History

Alexander, G. "The Natural History of High Altitudes." *Biology* 33:3:91-97.

Bengtson, K.E. "Coleman Glacier Studies, Mount Baker." *Mountaineer* 13:36-7.

Burke, Raymond. "Neoglaciation of Boulder Valley, Mount Baker, Washington." Masters thesis, Western Washington State College, 1972.

Daubenmire, R.F. "Ecologic Plant Geography of the Pacific Northwest." *Madroño* 20:3:111-28.

Davidson, George. "Recent Volcanic Activity in the United States." *Science* 6:262.

Dyson, James L. *The World of Ice.* New York: Alfred A. Knopf, 1962.

Easterbrook, Don J., and Rahm, David A. *Landforms of Washington.* Bellingham: Department of Geology, Western Washington State College, 1970.

Edwards, Ola. "Adaptation to Harshness: Alpine Plants in the Pacific Northwest." *Mountaineer* 48:57.

English, Edith Hardin. "Mammals of Austin Pass, Mt. Baker." *Mazama* 12:2:34-43.

Fries, Mary A. *Wildflowers of Mount Rainier and the Cascades.* Seattle: The Mountaineers and Mount Rainier Natural History Association, 1970.

Harris, Stephen L. *Fire and Ice: The Cascade Volcanoes.* Seattle: The Mountaineers and Pacific Search Press, 1976.

Harrison, A.E. "Fluctuations of the Coleman Glacier, Mt. Baker, Washington." *Journal of Geophysical Research* 66:649-50.

——"Climate and Glacier Fluctuations." *American Geophysical Union Transactions* 45:608.

——"Short Notes on Fluctuations of Coleman Glacier, Mt. Baker, Washington, USA." *Journal of Glaciology* 9:393-6.

Hyde, Jack H., and Crandell, Dwight R. "Postglacial Volcanic Deposits of Mount Baker, Washington, and Potential Hazards from Future Eruptions." U.S. Geological Survey, Professional Paper 1022C, 1978.

Kozloff, Eugene N. *Plants and Animals of the Pacific Northwest.* Seattle: University of Washington Press, 1976.

Kritzman, Ellen B. *Little Mammals of the Pacific Northwest.* Seattle: Pacific Search Press, 1977.

Long, W.A. "Mount Baker's Disappearing Glacier." *Summit* 4:6.

Lyons, C.P. *Trees, Shrubs and Flowers to Know in Washington.* Toronto: J.M. Dent & Sons, 1956.

McKee, Bates. *Cascadia: The Geologic Evolution of the Pacific Northwest.* New York: McGraw-Hill, 1972.

Taylor, Ronald J., and Douglas, George W. *Mountain Wildflowers of the Pacific Northwest.* Portland: Binford and Mort, 1975.

Turekian, K.K., ed. *The Late Cenozoic Glacial Ages.* New Haven: Yale University Press, 1971.

Waitt, Richard B., Jr. "Evolution of Glaciated Topography of Upper Skagit Drainage Basin, Washington." *Arctic and Alpine Research* 9:2:185.

Wright, H.E., Jr., and Frey, D.G., eds. *The Quaternary of the United States.* Princeton: Princeton University Press, 1965.

Zwinger, Ann H., and Willard, Beatrice E. *Land Above the Trees.* New York: Harper and Row, 1972.

General History

Amoss, Pamela. "The Persistence of Aboriginal Beliefs and Practices Among the Nooksack Coast Salish." Ph.D. dissertation, University of Washington, 1972.

Avery, Mary W. *Washington: A History of the Evergreen State.* Seattle: University of Washington Press, 1965.

Clark, Ella F. *Indian Legends of the Pacific Northwest.* Berkeley: University of California Press, 1953.

Collins, June McCormick. *Valley of the Spirits: The Upper Skagit Indians of Western Washington.* Seattle: University of Washington Press, 1974.

Criswell, Harold C. "Historical Sketch: Mount Baker National Forest." *Mountaineer* 57:4:41-53.

DeBorde, Mary. "Glacier: A History." Glacier, Washington: Mount Baker-Snoqualmie National Forest, 1981 (mimeographed).

Easton, Charles Finley. "Mt. Baker, Its Trails and Legends." Bellingham: Whatcom Museum of History and Art (unpublished scrapbook), compiled 1903-1940.

Field, Newton. *The Mount Baker Almanac.* Bellingham: Mt. Baker National Forest, 1951 (mimeographed).

Hawley, Robert Emmett. *Skquee Mus: Pioneer Days on the Nooksack.* Bellingham: Whatcom Museum of History and Art, 1971.

Heller, Ramon. *Mount Baker Ski Area: A Pictorial History.* Bellingham: Mount Baker Recreation Company, 1980.

Howay, F.W.; Sage, W.N.; and Angus, H.F. *British Columbia and the United States.* Toronto: The Ryerson Press, 1942.

Jeffcott, Percival R. *Nooksack Tales and Trails.* Sedro-Woolley, Washington: Sedro-Woolley Courier Times, 1949.

―― *Cheechaco and Sourdough.* Bellingham: Pioneer Printing Company, 1963.

Johnson, Dorothy H., and Jeffcott, Percival R. *John A. Tennant: Early Pioneer and Preacher.* Bellingham: Fourth Corner Registry, 1978.

Judson, Katherine. *Myths and Legends of the Pacific Northwest.* Chicago: A.C. McClurg, 1910.

Majors, Harry M., ed. *Mount Baker: A Chronicle of Its Historic Eruptions and First Ascent.* Seattle: Northwest Press, 1978.

Meany, Edmond S. *History of the State of Washington.* New York: The Macmillan Company, 1910.

―― *Vancouver's Discovery of Puget Sound.* Portland: Binford and Mort, 1957.

Middleton, Lynn, *Place Names of the Pacific Northwest Coast.* Seattle: Superior Publishing Company, 1969.

Roe, JoAnn, *The North Cascadians.* Seattle: Madrona Publishers, 1980.

Roth, Lottie R. *History of Whatcom County.* Seattle: Pioneer Historical Publishing Company, 1926.

Smith, Marian W. "The Nooksack, the Chilliwack, and the Middle Fraser." *Pacific Northwest Quarterly* 41:330-41.

Stern, Bernhard J. *The Lummi Indians of Northwest Washington.* New York: Columbia University Press, 1934.

Tremaine, David G. "Indian and Pioneer Settlement of the Nooksack Lowland, Washington." Master's thesis, Western Washington State College, 1975.

Whitebrook, Robert Ballard. *Coastal Exploration of Washington.* Palo Alto: Pacific Books, 1959.

Willis, Margaret, ed. *Cheechacos All: The Pioneering of the Skagit.* Mount Vernon, Washington: Skagit County Historical Society, 1973.

Winthrop, Theodore. *The Canoe and the Saddle.* Tacoma: Williams, 1913.

Mountaineering History

Adams, W.C. "Reminiscences of Mt. Baker." *Mazama* 5:4:338-42.

Beckey, Fred. *Challenge of the North Cascades.* Seattle: The Mountaineers, 1969.

——— *Cascade Alpine Guide: Rainy Pass to Fraser River.* Seattle: The Mountaineers, 1981.

Cooper, Ed. "Climbing Notes: Mount Baker, Coleman Glacier Headwall." *Mountaineer* 51:4:101-2.

——— "Climbing Notes: Mount Baker, Roman Nose." *Mountaineer* 54:4:100.

Curtis, Asahel. "The Mountaineers' First Ascent of Mount Baker." *Mountaineer* 1:4:87-99.

Frazeur, Mrs. L.R. "With the Mountaineers in 1916." *Mountaineer* 9:7-24.

Jones, Chris. *Climbing in North America.* Berkeley: University of California Press, 1976.

McNeil, Fred H. "Backtracking Old Trails." *Mazama* 12:2:7-20.

Meany, Edmond S. "The Ascent of Mount Baker, 1919." *Mountaineer* 12:42-4.

Miles, John. "Mount Baker—1868." *Off Belay* 38:11-28.

——— "Prospectors and Mountaineers." *Off Belay* 38:11-28.

Nettleton, Lulie. "With the Mountaineers on Mount Baker." *Mountaineer* 1:4:88-96.

Parker, Jamieson. "The Mount Baker Outing of 1920." *Mazama* 6:1:3-15.

Rusk, C.E. *Tales of a Western Mountaineer.* Boston: Houghton Mifflin Company, 1924.

Scott, John D. *We Climb High.* Portland: The Mazamas, 1969.

Sholes, Gertrude Metcalfe. "The Mount Baker Outing of the Mazamas in 1909." *Mazama* 6:1:26-32.

Other Sources

Connelly, Dolly. "New Playground for 1960: Mount Baker's South Side." *Seattle Times,* November 29, 1959.

——— "Morovits: The Hospitable Hermit of Baker Lake." *Off Belay* 28:6-10.

——— "The Mount Baker Marathon." *Off Belay* 7:2-7.

Frome, Michael. *Whose Woods These Are.* Garden City, New Jersey: Doubleday & Company, Inc., 1962.

Hazard, Joseph T. *Snow Sentinels of the Pacific Northwest.* Seattle: Lowman & Hanford Co., 1932.

LaChapelle, Dolores. *Earth Wisdom.* Los Angeles: The Guild of Tutors Press, 1978.

Moen, Wayne S. *Mines and Mineral Deposits of Whatcom County, Washington.* Olympia: State of Washington, Department of Natural Resources, 1969.

Mount Baker Club Scrapbooks, 1930-1970.

Parke, William N. "Report on the 1939 Mount Baker Avalanche Rescue Work." Washington: Government Printing Office, 1940.

Sucher, David, ed. *The Asahel Curtis Sampler.* Seattle: Puget Sound Access, 1973.

Tobias, Michael Charles, and Drasdo, Harold, eds. *The Mountain Spirit.* Woodstock, New York: The Overlook Press, 1979.

U.S. Forest Service. "Analysis of National Forest Lands Included in a Proposal for a North Cascades National Park." Portland: Pacific Northwest Region, December 1962.

U.S. Forest Service. *Highlights in the History of Forest Conservation.* Washington: Government Printing Office, 1976.

U.S. Forest Service. "Report on the Recreation Resources of the National Forests in the North Cascades." Portland: Pacific Northwest Region, 1963.

U.S. Forest Service. "Summary, Final Environmental Statement, Roadless Area Review and Evaluation." Washington, D.C.: Government Printing Office, 1979.

U.S. Department of Interior and Department of Agriculture, North Cascades Study Team. *The North Cascades.* Washington, D.C.: Government Printing Office, 1965.

U.S. National Park Service and Western Washington University. *The North Cascades: An Environmental Symposium.* Bellingham: Western Washington University, 1976.

Index

PHOTO CREDITS

ABOUT THE AUTHOR:

John C. Miles, a resident of Bellingham, Washington, has a closeup view of Mount Baker backdropping the city on every clear day. He first climbed the mountain in 1968, and has been back up to the summit eleven times since, by four routes. Fascinated by the mountain's history and its relationship to the people of the Northwest, Miles has made study of the mountain and exploring its environs his major avocation. He has also climbed extensively in the Washington and Oregon Cascades, the Olympics, B.C. Coast Range, Wind River Range, and Tetons.

Miles is an associate professor at the Huxley College of Environmental Studies at Western Washington University, Bellingham. He holds a bachelor's degree in anthropology from Dartmouth, a master's in recreation and park management from the University of Oregon, and a doctorate in education from Union Graduate School, Cincinnati. He has published a number of articles in mountaineering and conservation magazines in addition to scholarly journals; this is his first book.

Other books from The Mountaineers include:

MOUNTAIN NAMES, by Robert Hixson Julyan. An A-to-Z compilation of the stories behind the names of more than 300 of the world's most famous mountains, plus obscure peaks with marvelous monikers.

H.W. TILMAN: The Seven Mountain-Travel Books. A one-volume, unabridged collection of these rare, out-of-print titles: *Snow on the Equator, The Ascent of Nanda Devi, When Men and Mountains Meet, Mount Everest 1938, Two Mountains and a River, China to Chitral, Nepal Himalaya.*

THE CHALLENGE OF RAINIER, by Dee Molenaar. First complete documentation of the climbing history of Mt. Rainier. Many first-hand accounts; photos, sketches.

MT. McKINLEY: The Pioneer Climbs, by Terris Moore. Highlights of climbs on North America's highest peak, from initial explorations into the 1940s.

MONTE CRISTO, by Philip R. Woodhouse. Complete history, from discovery in 1889 through the mining boom-and-bust to today's tourist site, of this ghost town in Cascades.

SNOQUALMIE PASS: From Indian Trail to Interstate, by Yvonne Prater. Lavishly illustrated history of the busy highway pass through the Cascades as a gateway to Puget Sound.

LOOKOUTS: Firewatchers of the Cascades and Olympics, by Ira Spring and Byron Fish. Photos and fascinating tales of the hundreds of forest fire lookouts built throughout the mountains of Washington over 30 years, and of the people who lived in them.

Write for illustrated catalog of more than 100 titles:

The Mountaineers • Books
715 Pike St., Seattle, Wa 98101
(206) 682-4636